Okay God,
Let's Talk

Lyn Levine

Okay God, Let's Talk

By Lyn Levine

This book is dedicated to
those who seek love and laughter

Foreword
By Arlette Parker

I met Lyn about thirty years ago. My 17-year-old son was a walking upset and most of his anger was directed at me. A friend suggested that I see Lyn and so off we went, my son and I. In one hour she shook our realities with a mixture of loving instinct, scolding (both of us), processes, recreating each other and importantly, laughter. I was hooked. In a few sessions my son and I were back on track.

Trust, which doesn't come easily with me, has been a hallmark of our thirty-year relationship. She has never let me down, disappointed me or not been available. And I know that I am simply one of many she helps while simultaneously juggling multiple projects – this woman is impressive.

So, what makes her different and trustworthy right from the get go? Her propensity to love and her commitment to making a difference seems part of her DNA. She has a creative mind and able to create as she speaks. Over the years she has gotten me out of trouble, empowered and supported every one of my projects making even the dubious possible. When she coaches me I run with the ball without question.

I am thrilled Lyn has written a book teaching us that life is lived in the present moment. She has created a guide book for transforming fear into love. For me this book is precious and priceless.

Arlette

Introduction
By Lyn Levine

I did what I thought I was supposed to do to be happy. I married, had a house, children and a career. But I wasn't happy. If getting what I wanted didn't make me happy, I was doomed to keep going after something I thought would make me happy. Once I got what I wanted, I wouldn't be any happier than I was before. I finally figured out I didn't know how to be happy. I went on a quest to discover the secret of happiness.

In researching happy people, two ingredients emerged. The first was they completed their past, healing old wounds. If not healed, past wounds will be repeated today with other people. I did and do whatever I can to complete my past.

The other ingredient was believing in something larger than ourselves that was loving. Happy people believed in a higher power, or God, that loved them and was available for support. The problem was I no longer believed in the existence of an eternal being. I solved the problem by creating my own, do-it-yourself-God. I called him Bernie. He was my personal God who loved and supported me. Bernie's job was to enjoy me and think my faults were cute.

My job was to let in Bernie's love and support. I started having conversations with him. I enjoyed experiencing his love and acceptance of me, and we developed our relationship. I started to trust that his love was permanent and nonjudgmental. To remind me I was loved I developed connections with nature, imagining trees saying, "*I love you Lyn.*" When leaves and branches were moving, they were waving to me. Flowers were telling me "*Hello Lyn! You're adored, feel good!*"

And Birds! When I saw or heard a bird sing, they were singing to me. And clouds. I added children, and animals and smiles. Double numbers made me smile, and triple numbers made me laugh. I started filling up my love tank.

One day someone asked if I believed in God, and I didn't want to sound weird by saying I believed in Bernie, so I said yes. After that I called him God.

Introduction
By Lyn Levine

My relationship with God was somewhere between a wise, experienced friend, and a divine being who had nothing else to do but be available to me. He was an inexpensive therapist. While I was working things out he was patient and accepting, giving me permission to be petty and critical. His love was so unconditional, I knew there was nothing I could do to have him not love me. It gave me permission to be kinder to myself and others.

Years ago, I started writing down some of our conversations. I wrote out a booklet with some of our conversations, and gave some away. One recipient said she left my booklet on her coffee table and she, and her two children who attended Christian schools, would open to any page and it would help them with issues they were having in life. Another time, I emailed the manuscript to a friend who was struggling. He said none of the pages, except for one came through, and that one page seemed meant for him and changed his life. Experiment by turning to any page and see if it's for you.

This book has three intentions. The first is sharing what worked for me to be happy. I found that believing in the existence of God, and at the same time, doubt and question his existence, worked for me. I was able to create, accept and discover a trusting relationship that could, at the same time, contain cynicism.

The second reason for sharing is that in some ways I am an example of what's possible. As of this writing, I am 85 years old and feel ageless. In my 50's, my body was getting stiff and achy, and I had some physical conditions. I needed to stretch to get out of bed. Today I wake up like a child, delighted to be alive, without aches or pains or stiffness. As time went on my physical conditions disappeared.

Our bodies have 37 trillion cells, which are constantly being created. When loved and appreciated, our cells show off their vitality and health.

Introduction
By Lyn Levine

When I realized I could create anything, I declared "*I am always well.*" I became a warrior for wellness, believing I was well. When I had symptoms, I knew they were temporary and that new cells would produce perfect health. Yes, from time to time I get sick, and I know it is temporary. I use symptoms as an invitation to let go of something not joyful.

I also declared "*I am always young.*" Maybe aging is a conversation. Mind over matter. I decline to decline. Since my body's cells are always being replaced with new ones, I welcome them with a young spirit, and a delighted-to-be-alive attitude.

As I decreased struggle and suffering, and increased feeling good, I made it official by declaring "*I am always happy.*"

My third reason is to share what I discovered about being happy, healthy and youthful. Through my psychotherapy practice, leading seminars and living a life of varied interests, I have been committed to supporting others in their health and happiness. When I say, "*If I can do it, so can you,*" sometimes people say, "*Good for you, but tell me how.*" These conversations are samples of how I trained my mind to think healthy, young and happy.

The "Lyn" that speaks to God is sometimes me, and sometimes representative of others, or perhaps what an average person would say. I wanted to share the secrets one of us discovered during a lifetime of searching for how to feel good in the game of life.

Love,

Lyn Levine

Page 1

Lyn: I think I'm a shopper in life.

God: Say more.

Lyn: When I'm with you, and connected with love, I'm aware and delighted. When I'm not, I search for something.

God: Keep going.

Lyn: I shop for clothes, or food or entertainment. I shop for something that will make me feel good. But that's temporary. I shop by looking through my phone or computer for something interesting, or agrees with what I already believe. I shop to look good, or feel good or sound good, or pass as good.

God: You're on to something.

Lyn: If feeling good is outside-based, I can become addicted to an object or person or thing or feeling. I then need more and more of it. If feeling good is all outward-bound, my world is limited and unsafe. I develop a habit of being needy and dependent. Or lonely. Or depressed. Or resigned.

God: When are you not a shopper in life?

Lyn: When I've practiced feeling good enough, it becomes a new habit. I then live in a world that's safe and generous. Life is on my side and enjoys me just the way I am, and the way I am not. I either belong in a loving world, or I'm a shopper for love, safety and belonging.

God: What is possible?

Lyn: I'm letting go of a *fear-based, not-good-enough* view. I look for the good, not the bad. I see what works, not what's broken. I notice we're doing the best we can, given our view of ourselves. I trust life is a gift for my benefit and I enjoy freedom and power. I'm a devotee of love, peace, joy and gratitude.

Page 2

Lyn: I've been thinking about how upsets are reminders of incomplete wounds from the past.

God: Nice.

Lyn: When we're happy, we don't store anything. When unhappy we store our disappointments, resentments, hurt feelings, and upsets. We have visiting rights to suffering.

God: Keep going.

Lyn: Past wounds, particularly childhood wounds, want to be completed. They lie in wait, like a heat-seeking missile, until a similar situation arises. For instance, if our father wasn't nurturing, we can be upset over today's male not being nurturing. We usually don't get to the original source of our father's neglect, forgiving him and taking a kinder view, because we think we're upset over today's person.

God: Say more.

Lyn: We discard today's person, only to grab a new person, who turns out to be another insufficient nurturer. Maybe love is the answer. Loving, not looking for love.

God: What could work?

Lyn: Upsets are often reminders of unresolved past incidents. The feelings and emotions are the same as the original wound. We can examine upsets as snapshots from yesterday.

God: What else?

Lyn: When upset, we can ask ourselves what this reminds us of in the past, and willingly forgive and complete. Taking kinder views can soften or release the upset. When I'm upset, after I calm down I ask myself how it makes me feel about myself, and what that reminds me of in the past. I can then forgive or reframe. Maybe all upsets are from the past.

Page 3

Lyn: Sometimes when I'm talking with you , you ask me to work it out, That's okay if I have the time and patience, or even interest, but sometimes I just want an answer. Now!

God: What else?

Lyn: I'm surprised when you don't answer my questions. I know why that is. If I figure it out myself, I'll own it. Otherwise I'm just a gatherer of information.

God: What else.

Lyn: When I'm involved in something I'm connected, even inspired. When involved, it's a game worth playing. Or, I'm an outsider, involved with temporary distractions.

God: Sounds good to me.

Lyn: When I talk with you I get to question and answer, and figure out. Puzzles or mysteries require some participation on my part. I bring myself into the mix as an investment. Any time I have something at stake I'm more involved.

God: Say more.

Lyn: Although I want you to answer my questions, the downside is I might have less interest in your answer than when I figure things out. When I discover, I'm enriched. The pathway to being inspired is to be interested or connected. Life is a game of participation. Observers can be confused or disconnected. Even resigned. With you, I'm connected.

God: What makes my presence powerful for you?

Lyn: It's your love and acceptance. I'm like a child, able to express herself, play, perform, be hurt, and it's all okay. You give me permission to be, and an invitation to express. With nothing to lose and everything to gain.

Page 4

Lyn: One of my sons severely injured his ankle. I strongly believe in the power of prayer and visualization. I'm committed to his perfect healing. I can picture him quickly healed. But sometimes I start to worry, and I know worry is in alignment with fear.

God: All is proceeding perfectly, no matter what it looks like. Upsets over what happens has you swimming against the current, rather than flowing with the way things are. Your reaction is saying *no* to life.

Lyn: Hold on! One of mine got hurt. You'd better believe that's a big *NO* in my world. Yes, the world I live in is now endangered. And yes, I've left the sweet confidence of letting you guide me, and put fear between us.

God: I don't join you in fear. Only love.

Lyn: Even though I'm creating fear—and feel justified—the biggest gift I can give my son is to turn his life over to you and trust that all is well, no matter what. I ask you to take away my fear and let me feel loved and safe. I turn his health over to you, and trust that his highest good is happening. I ask you to support me in connecting to your love and guidance. I ask you for the courage to believe and stand for his perfect healing.

God: I accept.

Lyn: Thank you. I would say "*God bless you*" except that doesn't make sense.

God: Your thanks will do. And thank you for being an example of calm when fear is so inviting.

Lyn: Thank you for showing that love is needed most in urgent times. I choose to remember and trust you.

Page 5

Lyn: My son's ankle is healing. Thank you for reminding me it's not what happens—but my reaction to what happens—that makes a difference. Thank you for your support.

God: You're welcome.

Lyn: because of our relationship, I can accept what happens in life much more than I did in the past.

God: Acceptance makes life easier.

Lyn: I can connect with you and feel loved and safe when all goes well. When I'm frightened, it's more difficult to trust that things will work out the way I want. When I feel at risk, I picture the worst that might happen, and become even more fearful, imaging the worst.

God: What is faith?

Lyn: The dictionary says that faith is having unquestioning belief. How can I not question when bad results happen?

God: How would you like our relationship to be when you're frightened?

Lyn: I'd like to turn my fear over to you, and ask you to let me feel safe with whatever happens. If I can only trust you when I get what I want, I'm going to be alone with my fear.

God: Good insight.

Lyn: I did keep connecting with you during my son's condition. I kept turning my fear over to you, trading it in for love and trust. It worked—most of the time. You're certainly an amazing antidote to anxiety and upset. And my calmness was useful to others involved. You really are a great investment.

God: I'm always here.

Lyn: I'm trying not to be silly by saying "Thank God for you."

Page 6

Lyn: I'm either doing what I said I'm going to do, or I'm not! I'm either doing what I think I should be doing, or I'm not! Who am I arguing with? Who am I in conflict with?

God: Keep going.

Lyn: I'm not sure who is running my life. Is it me, or my wants? You and I are running my life when I feel good. A damaged, frightened child is running my life when I feel bad. And you can't help me out when I'm frightened because I'm closed off and defended. When I need you the most, you can't help me. It seems like you're only there for the good times.

God: I'm there when you connect with love, when you come from thoughts that make you feel good, from actions that make you feel good, from words that make you and others feel good.

Lyn: What about the dark side?

God: I can't join you in the dark side, because there isn't any dark side for me. I created you out of love, and if you are creating out of fear, separation and suffering, it is an illusion. You can live in it—like a nightmare—but it doesn't exist. I cannot go where love is absent. You need to join me.

Lyn: Now you tell me!

God: I often tell you.

Lyn: Why is it always my fault?

God: You're the one complaining.

Lyn: I can't win with you.

God: You've already won with me.

Lyn: Okay, I give up. Maybe I'll surrender to your love.

God: How about surrendering to your love.

Lyn: Hmm. Maybe I'll simply allow love.

Page 7

Lyn: I don't want to stop the anger. I'm entitled to it! I have proof I should be angry. Letting go seems like a weakness, a giving in, a victim.

God: Say more.

Lyn: Oh, I just saw something! I'm angry because I feel victimized, and yet letting go of the anger also feels like I'm victimized. How can that be?

God: Can you make any sense out of this?

Lyn: Yes, I think I can. When I'm scared I disconnect from you, and all of life. It's like I'm drowning while trying to grab onto something for support. I'm frightened and alone. Anger appears as something strong to hold onto. Anger has more power than depression or sadness.

God: What else?

Lyn: Let me try and work this out. Maybe I'm afraid I'll blame myself if I stop my outward blame. Maybe anger is really an antidote to sadness. Okay, that sounds right. I'm now able to relate with you more, and able to relate with the part of me that is willing to let go of the anger.

God: As your anger subsides, what becomes available?

Lyn: Choice. I am slowly gaining the possibility of choice. I can see other sides of what happened. I am more able to choose to continue the anger, or to let go. Choosing the anger seems more powerful than being buried in it. Interesting. Before I had no choice. There was only anger.

God: Good work.

Lyn: I don't know what to do when I'm sad, but I sure know how to keep the story going when I'm angry. Maybe I can accept that sometimes I am sad. When angry, maybe I could ask if I'm sad or mad. I'm going to keep inquiring about the relationship between sad and mad.

Page 8

Lyn: How can I have inner quiet?

God: Inner quiet is a space to be maintained. Like a garden or a calm sanctuary, it requires structures of support.

Lyn: Okay. I could say "*cancel*" to a negative thought and replace it with a kind statement. I can say "*all is well*" like a mantra throughout the day. I could count my blessings. Appreciation works.

God: Good.

Lyn: Except I'm usually at the mercy of random thoughts of fears from the past and fears of the future.

God: Past brain-patterns are running you.

Lyn: Maybe getting better is just improvement, rather than a creation. I'm fixing a broken past. I could create I am quiet.

God: Say more.

Lyn: Instead of looking outside for inner quiet, I can create that inner quiet already exists, and just relax into it.

God: Nice.

Lyn: Now that I'm thinking inner quiet exists, maybe it's something I can just allow. I can enjoy feeling the calm effects of inner peace and quiet. I can set aside time to practice and enjoy inner quiet. I guess that's what some people call meditation. Maybe meditation is simply allowing the mind to quiet down.

God: Maybe.

Lyn: I know prayer is talking to you. Perhaps meditation can be listening to you.

God: Creating you was a good idea.

Lyn: Creating you was a good idea.

Page 9

Lyn: I had an argument with someone, and I'm distancing myself from them. I'm justifying it by telling myself I'm choosing to remain separate. I suspect I'm being righteous. I don't want to renew the relationship. I think I want to be mad. I also think it's bad to be mad and should forgive.

God: You should be mad.

Lyn: Now you're playing with me. You should teach me how not to be mad. You should teach me to be more loving.

God: Let's see. You want to be mad, but think if you were a good person you would forgive and reconnect.

Lyn: Well, yes, that's about right.

God: If you can, accept where you are since that's where you are. It's all okay. It's the best you can do given how life occurs for you. If you can relax and accept, you can shift into a kinder reality. If you can accept being there, you'll grow into yet another, more peaceful place. If you can't accept where you are, you are stuck in that place.

Lyn: If I'm unhappy, and think "*I should be happy*" I stay in unhappiness longer than if I accept that I'm unhappy. Right?

God: If you accept being unhappy for now, you can move on at your own pace. If you think unhappiness is wrong, you are at war with the way it is. What you resist, persists.

Lyn: If I choose to stay mad for now, it's okay. That does feel better. You might be on to something. Does it bother you that I keep learning and forgetting the golden rule?

God: Nothing bothers me. You all do what you do, like treasured children in a playground. What would it be like for you to live like you were adored?

Lyn: I'd be free and powerful and creative, with sweetness and laughter and abundance and love.

Page 10

Lyn: Just how much feeling good is a person supposed to have? I feel good sometimes, but not all the time. I was wondering if there was a grading system, like A, B or C, for measurement.

God: What grade or rating would you like?

Lyn: Maybe I'd like assurance or acknowledgment. If I got an A, I would argue that I'm not that good. If I got a B, I'd ask how to become an A. If I got rated C, I'd feel ordinary. If I got a D, I'd feel inadequate. If I got an F, I'd be resigned. It's a silly question. I'm searching for answers.

God: What's the difference between searching and finding?

Lyn: When I'm searching there's an urgency in finding a solution. Safety is missing. When I'm exploring, I'm curious and interested. I can enjoy it the experience. Searching can be for finding, while exploring can be to discover.

God: Say more.

Lyn: When I forget about you, I can feel trapped and look for a way out. Once I connect with you I'm safe, and can handle life without the fear of survival or approval.

God: With love you're safe at home.

Lyn: You're the antidote to the unending puzzle of being human. I know I'm growing, because I feel stuck for shorter lengths of time, and safe for longer intervals.

God: It's good to have you home more often.

Lyn: I spend time struggling to figure out life and how to be happy. You live at home, in love. I live mostly in *not-there-yet*. Not much peace in that view.

God: Move to the land of love.

Lyn: Inside the world of survival, my suffering and scarcity seem ordinary. Love leads to extraordinary. A better deal.

Page 11

Lyn: I think a good person is someone who does your commandments, follows the golden rule, is kind and loving.

God: Sounds good to me. How does it sound to you?

Lyn: Like I'm falling way short of that mark.

God: I created you as perfect. You're still working it out. I view your antics and dramas as a loving parent watching a young child. You make mistakes and spend more time with guilt and shame than with me.

Lyn: Can you throw a bone of advice to this silly human?

God: Clean up your supply of guilt and shame. Forgive. See a kinder view. Admit your vulnerability. Tell the truth. Be responsible. Or, keep hiding behind the pretense of being good while feeling bad.

Lyn: I do sometimes think I'm bad.

God: You don't accept that you're loved because you think you're not worth loving. Then you waste your life trying to prove you *are* worth loving. Even special.

Lyn: Oh. Wow. I asked for a bone and you gave me a hammer. That's a lot to think about. It helps a little to know I'm the source of my suffering with all my guilt and shame. I'm glad I believe in you. You're a life-preserver in an ocean of fear and chaos.

God: What would your life be like if you believed you were forgiven and loved?

Lyn: I would enjoy the beauty and magnificence of a world created for me, your loved child. I would be delighted with the wonders of nature and the variety of others as playmates. I would see everything as a gift from you. I'd be happy and fulfilled. Or, I can keep proving I'm inadequate.

Page 12

Lyn: I want to be a better person, but keep resisting practices that make me better. I want to be thin, but eat what's fattening. I want to be organized, but resist putting things away and finishing tasks. I want to help the environment, but consume and discard mindlessly.

God: Is it your goal or your actions or your guilt and shame that bothers you?

Lyn: Didn't see that they are separate. Well, for sure, guilt and shame are the hardest to bear. If I could just live the way I feel like living, I'd be good enough for me, for now.

God: I give you permission to live the way you are living.

Lyn: No. That's not the way it should be. I should be better. Boy, what a trap. Thinking I should be better than I am leaves me a failure. Okay, I get it. I am the way I am. You give me permission to be the way I am, with faults and weaknesses, and you love me anyway. Come to think of it, maybe that really is unconditional love.

God: I do love you unconditionally. I don't need or want you to be better. I like you just the way you are. You are precious to me as-is. Don't change for any reason other than if that's what you want.

Lyn: Okay, I'm taking on being me and enjoying being me. When I'm happy I tend to take care of myself and others. I tend to follow practices that serve my needs anyway. And have a good time doing them. And never wonder if I'm a good or bad person. Being happy is not personal.

God: Nice.

Lyn: I think so too. When my identity is in charge, I'm pretending to be a good person. When disconnected from love, life's a struggle and punishment. When I'm being present, I'm happy and generous, enjoying being alive.

Page 13

Lyn: I've been pretending that everything that happens is a gift from you, and it's been great. I'm enjoying the experience of being loved and safe like a beloved child.

God: Why do you pretend I love you and take care of you?

Lyn: I want so much to believe it but I'm afraid I'm making this whole thing up. I think I'm making up that you exist, and that we speak, and that I'm safe and loved. I'm afraid this might be all in my imagination.

God: Let's say, for now, that you *are* making me up.

Lyn: Oh well, if I knew for sure I'm making you up, I'm certainly going to continue to do so, since it really serves me. I'm not going to stop believing in you.

God: It works for you to believe in me, but you are unable to trust that I exist outside of your creation.

Lyn: I don't want to stop believing in you. Yet, I don't know how to trust that you're real, and talking to little me.

God: Believing when you believe and doubting when you doubt are fine with me. How about making it fine with you? Love accepts it all.

Lyn: Okay. I can accept that you exist and that I sometimes doubt the whole thing. And that I forget about you for big pieces of time.

God: Maybe love has the freedom to be expressed in many ways, and can be different at different times.

Lyn: Really? I'm feeling so much better. Now I can have unloving thoughts about you and still believe I'm loved.

God: You can always count on my love.

Lyn: I can see it is my love that can't be counted on. I don't like being a fickle lover.

Page 14

Lyn: Today I was with a woman who was complaining about being unloved. I told her I loved her. I asked if she could allow herself to experience that love. After a quiet moment, she felt the love that was available. It occurred to me that maybe love is a flow.

God: Love is your birthright. You are always connected to love. You are the one who disconnects and becomes the source of your own suffering and separation.

Lyn: You're in my world when I'm happy or appreciating, like a playmate. When I'm needy or frightened, I reach out to you for support like you have the supply of what I need.

God: Say more.

Lyn: When I feel good, I'm not missing anything. I belong. All is well. You and I are powerful and equal. When frightened, or confused or overwhelmed, I become insufficient, inadequate, small and helpless.

God: I like this.

Lyn: I just saw something. I can only experience being loved when I'm loving. Otherwise I'm located outside the warmth of love, shivering in the cold. You are not just my God, but my best friend. Being your playmate has us both owning all of life and enjoying the experience.

God: You are perfect and amazing just as you are, just as you were, and as you will be. Thank you for our partnership. Those who can *lighten up*, can light the path for others, who light the path for still others. Candles lighting candles.

Lyn: When I'm appreciative or joyful, I lighten up. Love is always available. Whenever and wherever I look, love can be discovered. Love is really the ingredient that fuels eternal light. I hope I can remember this tomorrow.

Page 15

Lyn: I keep forgetting our relationship. I forget I'm loved and all is well. On my own I'm like a child living a soap opera. I dishonor your love when I think I'm bad or selfish or lazy. I have been remembering you more lately, and it's a wonderful circuit-breaker when I get upset. Love works.

God: Nice observation.

Lyn: I've been wondering what love is. If I say, *"I love you"* without experiencing it, am I lying? Sometimes I tell people I love them without feeling the love at that moment. I guess it's to reassure people. Or—and I hate to admit this—it's to keep them close. Some wise person said love was accepting another just the way they are.

God: When is love experienced?

Lyn: When I feel a sweetness for someone, telling them I love them is a natural expression of that love. There's no *reason* for doing it. There's nothing in it for me, or for them, other than to express how I'm feeling. I guess when it's real, I'm sharing love. Otherwise I'm just talking about it without feeling, like a concept.

God: How do you know I love you?

Lyn: Oh, I just know it. Your love for me is a done deal that cannot be damaged. You love me because a loving God loves completely. I am responsible for knowing I'm loved.

God: Well done. You're always loved.

Lyn: If I'm always loved, I'm the one who is responsible for knowing I'm always loved, especially when I feel unlovable. When my identity says I'm not worth loving I can plug into your love, like a machine plugging into electricity. Thanks for loving me. And by the way, I love you.

Page 16

Lyn: Right now, I'm not feeling good about myself or life. I don't like me, or even you, for that matter.

God: You're not connecting to your inner source of love.

Lyn: I don't want to be a pretend person that goes around acting like everything is fine.

God: How can I help you?

Lyn: I want you to tell me how to stop feeling bad and to feel good. Can you be a nice God and do that for me?

God: Do you have any suggestions on how I might help you?

Lyn: No. Do you?

God: Are you willing to be happy?

Lyn: How can I be happy when I don't know if I'm depressed or upset or angry or frightened?

God: Love is available when seen through loving eyes.

Lyn: Okay. I can see that I've been living through angry fearful eyes, seeing what's wrong and bad. If you let me I could complain about everything. Life seems unfair and uncaring.

God: What's possible?

Lyn: I know it's possible to feel good except it feels like an uphill climb. I want to be *right* about feeling bad. I keep thinking about all the reasons to feel bad.

God: You have my permission to feel bad and it doesn't make you a bad person.

Lyn: Feeling bad follows a reason to feel bad. At least I now know I'm growing because of the certainty that love awaits my return, instead of thinking I'm doomed for life.

God: Feeling bad is useful in providing the contrast of what you don't want to be able to create what you do want.

Page 17

Lyn: Most of use seem to be waiting to get what we want.

God: Keep waiting.

Lyn: What is the source of all that waiting?

God: Not knowing that *now* is the point of power. There is only now. All *is* the way it is. You either vote for it or against it. One gives you freedom, the other bondage.

Lyn: Strange then, how we think time will give us what we want. We act as if we are powerless to alter anything, especially since we spend so much energy suffering over all of our reasons to suffer.

God: Energy flows where attention goes. You'd rather be right about why you're not happy than be happy. Whatever you pay attention to increases like seeds being watered. Shall I go on?

Lyn: No, you made your point. The point you keep making, no matter what the topic.

God: And you seem to leave joy for struggle, no matter anything.

Lyn: Do you get impatient with us?

God: For heaven's sake, of course not. You're the best game in town. It's interesting to watch you, especially when you ask for my help. You ask when the mess you created is so strongly held in place by your feelings and conversations, little support can get through.

Lyn: I forget that you gave us free will and we create fear and helplessness. You can't join us there. I seem to own two homes: one a defended fort and one with open doors.

God: I join you in love, in connection, in joy, in peace, in laughter, in creation, in contributing, in appreciation.

Lyn: Joining you has the best of me show up. I choose joy.

Page 18

Lyn: I'm disappointed that confidence or certainty doesn't remain stable for any length of time. Feeling good lasts until interrupted by negativity or fear.

God: Be grateful that times of despair are not permanent.

Lyn: I do see the bright side often, especially when others complain. I'm usually unwilling to go into their dark side. When I monitor myself, I can resist fear and complaint.

God: Accepting that others suffer without having to suffer as well is loving. Both of you are supported.

Lyn: Does fear invite more fear? Oh, I'll answer that. It does. As soon as someone starts complaining others join in with their own complaints. It becomes almost a contest to see who knows the most frightening stories.

God: What are examples of good talk?

Lyn: Sometimes when I hear someone complain about another, I'll say, I think they like you. The effect is magical. The complainer is relieved somewhat, and the complaint softens.

God: Any other tips?

Lyn: When someone complains about me, I can say, "I see that you're upset with me," and "I'd like to apologize. Please tell me what I can apologize for." And listen to what they say, without arguing. I'm able to get into their world, and see how they see the situation. I can speak to their reality and say, "I can see how what I did or said, or didn't do or say, made you feel hurt, or rejected or angry," and, coming from love, gently form an apology from not realizing their interpretation. All we want is to be heard, known and understood, which is more important than being right that someone is wrong. Once we're connected I can share my view. If I defend, telling them they are wrong when they are upset, it escalates the upset. We're both victimized.

Page 19

Lyn: When I'm being the person you created me to be I am you, loving and accepting. When I am who I created me to be I'm *not-good-enough* trying to prove I'm worth loving.

God: Say more.

Lyn: Anything can be enriching if I choose it. I can choose this time, this place, this moment. I can be here, tasting food, appreciate the wonder of having a body, the wonder of nature, discovering the majesty of life.

God: Nice.

Lyn: Creation allows choice. Identity is fixed. Am I feeling good or feeling bad? When I do choose to be me as I am, I'm good enough. When I'm not the one choosing, I exist in a default life, as if the world will somehow motivate my interest and passion. I use drug-like habits to fill up my sentence until rescued or eliminated.

God: Before you get too depressed, what is possible? Will this conversation matter in your moment by moment existence?

Lyn: I can take your hand and walk my path with your guidance. Thank you for creating me as perfect. I choose to remember you and feel cuddled in your love. My best wake-up call is talking to you and knowing I'm loved and safe.

God: Nice.

Lyn: I'll go through my day saying *thank you*, seeing my day full of gifts. I will write in my gratitude journal, as an empowered person, instead of a victim. If love is who I am, I can simply allow lovingness. I can see lovingly, hear lovingly, think lovingly, speak lovingly and feel lovingly. Any of those connects me back to love.

God: Welcome home.

Page 20

Lyn: All there is, is love. Anything else is a waste of me. Why is it taking so long for me to get this?

God: You are easily distracted.

Lyn: Yes, that's true. I'm tempted by the false idols of possessions and approval. When I'm present, awake and aware, all is well. Everything else is trying to get to love, to get to success, to have my dreams come true. I leave *now*, where joy and wonder live, to look for joy and wonder outside of myself.

God: What has you choose outside fame and fortune over joy and wonder?

Lyn: It's a trap. The world of meanings and stories are way more seductive than the peace and quiet of wonder and joy. Everything outside of myself is designed to grab my attention, like a neon advertisement.

God: I suppose it's hopeless.

Lyn: Smart move. That got my attention. No way am I giving up or giving in. I have you to connect with, talk to and love. All I need is to make my connection with you more of a habit. A habit is just something I keep doing.

God: How can I support you?

Lyn: Keep sending signals to remind me you're there. Trees remind me of you. Children remind me of you. Clouds remind me of you. Flowers and colors and soft breezes remind me of you. Rain, singing birds, sunsets and sunrises remind me of you. Birds and animals remind me of you. Smiles and hugs and music remind me of you. You know, I might have enough reminders. I'll pay more attention.

God: Well done.

Lyn: All there is, is love. The purpose of love is to love.

Page 21

Lyn: I have a pile of papers on my desk I need to go through and am avoiding. There are things I need to handle that are time sensitive, and I still resist going through that pile. There are things I'm going to be punished for, and feel guilty about, and yet, I am not touching that pile of papers.

God: And the problem is?

Lyn: Haven't you had your coffee yet? Don't you understand that I really need to go through that pile or I'm in big trouble?

God: Would you like me to go through that pile with you?

Lyn: Oh. I never considered that. Are you sure you don't have something better to do—like stop wars, or end hunger?

God: Now that I'm looking at my calendar, it says, "*Support Lyn with paper pile*".

Lyn: See, now that I think I could go through that pile, with your help, I'm not sure that's what I want to do. I really don't want your help. I seem to be attached to resistance. Nobody and nothing can make me do what I don't want to do.

God: Take a deep breath.

Lyn: This is so powerfully dominating me it's hard to believe it's me talking. What happened to that nice happy person? I would love to have this kind of force in other areas of my life. There must be a way make friends with resistance. To resist is to fight against.

God: Keep going.

Lyn: I can pick up a paper on top of the pile and find it of interest, rather than a chore. I can set a time limit, and reward myself after a while. I can say, "*Please God, help me handle this,*" feeling free, safe and accomplished. Maybe I really can do it. That would be good.

God: Ask and receive.

Page 22

Lyn: Yesterday the effects on others seemed extraordinary. I was feeling good, and in my interactions with others, I could relate to their struggles with a loving simplicity that reduced the drama. "*What was so*" became *"So what!"*

God: What's the lesson here?

Lyn: Life shows up in the relationship between me and another or me and others. And sometimes when I'm present, really listening—and not mechanically relating to them to get through the moment—true connection is accomplished, and anything is possible. There are times I can create space for others to others.

God: I did a good job in creating you.

Lyn: That's a nice thing to say. The personal Lyn, not the *God connected Lyn,* is too small and insignificant to believe that my source—my creator—says he did a good job in creating me.

God: I did a good job in creating you.

Lyn: Okay, now I can sort it out, so that both my connected and disconnected selves can accept this. I can love myself and others even when we are neon signs flashing *imperfect* or *defective*. When we come from love you probably do think, (if God thinks) that you did a good job in creating us.

God: How did you work this out?

Lyn: I went outside of myself, and became present instead of a petty, insignificant unfinished Lyn, struggling with being too small and limited to allow for the richness of the moment to be. When we're connected I'm the wonderful space of all there is.

God: I did a good job in creating you.

Lyn: You could have made me a little taller.

Page 23

Lyn: I was with some people who were complaining.

God: What you don't like about yourself shows up in others.

Lyn: Yes, I feel bad when I'm whiny and complaining. Only when I do it, it seems more like an observation than a judgment.

God: What's the difference between observation and judgment?

Lyn: Observation is simply reporting, while judgment is giving an opinion. Yes, one is a neutral view and the other is voting on the good/bad scorecard.

God: What's another view of social conversations?

Lyn: Another view is others are divine beings doing the best they can, given their reality. If they feel stuck, they blame something or someone for being stuck.

God: Say more.

Lyn: When someone complains they reveal their restraints and helplessness. Being able to express their hurt and anger is easier than depression and despair.

God: How can you experience being with them?

Lyn: I can accept and love them. An outlet for frustration is to complain to anyone willing to listen, and hopefully, agree. I can simply accept that that's their view. I can admire their courage in dealing with the difficulty of that problem.

God: What else?

Lyn: I can resist telling them what to do. If I give my opinion, correction, or advice, I'll just show up as an authority figure, or a know-it-all. If appropriate, I could share how I handled a similar problem successfully. I could tell them I trust them to deal with the situation. I can simply appreciate them. My best gift to them is love them as is.

Page 24

Lyn: When do we need courage?

God: Whenever you have created fear.

Lyn: Created fear? Sometimes fear is appropriate.

God: Survival mechanisms are useful in dangerous situations. In ordinary times fear is just a habit.

Lyn: We are warned a lot growing up. Be careful of this, don't trust that, and beware of *those*. Our information highways bombard us with the latest violations and dangers. I do hold on to fearful thoughts. I avoid something or someone that's frightening s me, and can be afraid when something bad happens to someone else.

God: What's possible when afraid?

Lyn: There are times, though, when courage is useful. I can use courage to do something new, or to keep going when I want to quit. I can use courage to express myself when my views are unpopular, or when my actions are not ordinary. Maybe what I consider a lack of discipline, or lack of self-esteem, is simply a lack of courage.

God: What else could handle your fears?

Lyn: I could turn them over to you and know that I am safe. I could forgive myself and whatever I am afraid of. I could picture myself friends with what frightens me.

God: Nice.

Lyn: When I am feeling good, life is safe, and actions are appropriate. Then courage is not required. Again, love is the answer. When connected with you I take you with me on all journeys and tasks. You are my traveling companion.

God: Thank you for the courage to have this conversation.

Lyn: Thank you for trusting me to be courageous. And loving.

God: Thank you for being my partner in love.

Page 25

Lyn: Do other people relate to you, or are you my personal God? Do others have their own personal God? Are you a *one-size-fits-all-God*, or is there one for each of us? Although I think of you as my personal God, some other people think of you as one big source. Others think you are energy, or nature, or some ambiguous spirit or power.

God: Pick the interpretation or belief that is best for you. You like to wonder, whereas others like to be given a set of rules. Do what works for you for now. Later, do what works for you then. You can try to figure it out, or relax and let it be one of the mysteries of life.

Lyn: Okay. What works for me for now is that you are my personal God. You love me unconditionally and are always available. It works to know you're on my side and by my side. I'm glad I can have your time and support.

God: How can I support you?

Lyn: Knowing you're always there supports me. I have a little card, left over from Valentine's Day, that says *Be Mine*. I keep it on my desk. When I notice it I decide whether I want to be yours, or whether I want you to be mine.

God: What's the difference?

Lyn: If I am yours, I surrender to your loving view and just feel good. If you are mine, I'm asking for something for myself or others, or I turn things over to you. If I am yours, you're in charge. If you are mine, I'm in charge.

God: Interesting how you figured out choices in our relationship.

Lyn: I suspect you're one God in charge of it all, and I created you as my personal God because it's easier for me to relate to you. My guess is you don't care how I design you. You simply love and teach me to simply love. And to love simply.

Page 26

Lyn: Most people think there should be some purpose to life. Do we or don't we have a purpose in life?

God: It's fine if you have a purpose and it's fine if you don't.

Lyn: Most people want to be happy. Could that be a purpose?

God: Being happy means you're in alignment with life. Being happy feels free and powerful. All is well.

Lyn: Then being unhappy means something is wrong and should be fixed or improved. There's either a problem with us or with the world. With problems we're unhappy.

God: Say more.

Lyn: If my purpose in life is joy then I need to see life as being acceptable the way it was, the way it is, and the way it will be. Is seeing problems the source of unhappiness or is believing that problems exist the source of unhappiness?

God: What's the difference between believing there are problems and seeing problems?

Lyn: Oh, I see what you mean. They have the same result. When I'm happy life is a gift. Life is on my side. When I'm unhappy I see life as limited and threatening. I'm in survival and need to take care of myself. I see problems in people and in the world. It's reasonable for me to be unhappy.

God: What could work?

Lyn: Well, I could actually choose to be happy as a purpose in life. I could turn any reason I have for being unhappy over to you, clearing my plate for feeling good. Oh, and be here now in the present, not in my thoughts. That mindfulness stuff is smart. If I'm present, right now, it's a nice world that I get to play in. A sweet world. A world that has me feel at safe and loved, at home. Then, wherever I am, and whoever I'm with, I can be my authentic self and make a difference.

Page 27

Lyn: Does the world need my support? Does anyone?

God: No one needs you. If you choose to support something or someone, have a good time.

Lyn: Are you really saying there are essentially no problems that need my support, so no solutions are necessary? Am I just supposed to accept that life is evolving its own way? Then why am I here?

God: To ask that question.

Lyn: I suppose you think I'm just here to have a good time.

God: Basically, yes.

Lyn: It doesn't seem right to just accept life as it appears. Don't my opinions matter? Come to think about it, opinions are just voting for or against. Maybe peace is neutral territory. Hmm. Maybe taking sides is what arguments, fights and wars are all about.

God: Do I take sides?

Lyn: No. Love lets us be the way we are, without needing to be fixed or changed. Coming from love has us enjoy being alive wherever we are or whoever we're with.

God: Can I count on you to feel good?

Lyn: Maybe I *can* stop voting and let life be the way it is being. I can turn life over to you and ask to feel good.

God: What else?

Lyn: I could ask myself "*Am I feeling good?*" If the answer is no, I can take a kinder view of life.

God: What else?

Lyn: When I feel good, I'm loving and generous, and want others to feel good. Maybe feeling good is the way to peace.

Page 28

Lyn: It's commonly thought that aging brings decline. I find that trusting my body to be vital and healthy produces sweet results. Love works. Even my plants thrive when I love them.

God: Say more.

Lyn: I'd probably be physically declining if I wasn't in partnership with all my cells, especially those constantly being born. They show off their ability to produce perfect health, and I adore them with appreciation and gratitude.

God: Say more.

Lyn: If I do have a symptom, I don't make a big deal out of it, like I now have a problem. I trust my new cells are born perfect and those symptoms will soon disappear.

God: Say more.

Lyn: I have some old conversations that don't serve me. I'll hear my past voice telling me to take a jacket or I'll catch a cold, rather than to take a jacket in case I need it. I know better than to complain about my wonderful body. I no longer listen to people blame getting older as a source of their physical or mental problems. Fear produces more to fear. Appreciation produces more to appreciate.

God: Say more.

Lyn: My body is my precious pet and I treat it lovingly. I wake up in the morning hugging myself, enjoying the pleasure of being alive. I acknowledge my cells for being healthy warriors. In my 50's I used to wake up so stiff I felt rusty. I took on loving my body and knowing that new cells produce perfect health. Now, in my 80's, I'm grateful I created health and vitality. My body is my most important partnership, and I honor and enjoy our relationship.

God: Love can appear magical.

Page 29

Lyn: I figure about 100 pages is enough for this book.

God: Why are you writing this book?

Lyn: To share our relationship, conversations and insights as an example of what is possible.

God: For what reason?

Lyn: If people believe you're judgmental and punitive that's just more guilt, shame and fear. They then feel they deserve to struggle and suffer.

God: What's your concern?

Lyn: People will think I am making up what you say. Or, maybe I'm the one that thinks I'm probably making you up,

God: What if you are?

Lyn: What if I *am* making up what I think you would say? But sometimes I'm surprised at what you're saying. How can I be surprised if it's all me writing?

God: It could be you just being clever.

Lyn: Why can't it really be you I'm talking to? Maybe this doubting conversation is to put my mind at ease and let me know it's really you I'm talking to. And really, who cares?

God: Who are you trying to convince, you or me?

Lyn: I think it's you and me talking. But then again, maybe it's all you, and I'm just writing what you want me to write.

God: You can't seem to separate you from me.

Lyn: No, and I'm going to give up the questioning for now. Our relationship is the best gift I have, no matter what it is or who created it. Maybe I'm my own chemist mixing enough of ordinary life and other-worldliness together to make a magical formula for love, peace and joy.

Page 30

Lyn: I keep thinking I'm a good person who wants to make a difference with others, and I just saw how that isn't true. What's true is I want to be special. I want to be just a little better than everyone else, in areas that are important to me.

God: Good insight.

Lyn: There's nothing good about this insight. It's disgusting. How could I want to be better than others and say that I love people? It's that identity thing I become when I'm feeling unloved or a failure and then want to make up for it by standing out from the crowd.

God: How about being ordinary, capable of extraordinary results.

Lyn: Oh wow. That could work. I can be ordinary, not special, yet capable of producing special results.

God: Nice.

Lyn: When I feel good, I'm okay. I am home. All is well. It's only when I disconnect that I feel inferior, confused or upset. That's when I'm lost in struggle. When I'm not connected I'm sort of desperate to survive. That's when I need to be special.

God: Say more.

Lyn: When I feel good I want to contribute, not compete. I like being useful and making a difference. You are the antidote to surviving being human. You knew what you were doing when you created us. Although, and it's a little late to give you your instruction manual, you could have made us perfectly loving, without giving us free will. But then we wouldn't be playing this game of finding love, only to discover we've been loved all along. I think I'll give up improving you and improving me. At least for this page.

Page 31

Lyn: Sometimes I ask you for help when my resistance to receiving is practically super-glued in place. I think you have the power to plow through my inertia and make my dreams happen, even though I'm in the way.

God: This is just a conversation to you, and when you finish writing this page, you'll forget it. No real difference will be made.

Lyn: Well now, you're coming on a little strong about this. Are you annoyed with me?

God: You're the one who raised the issue of being unsupportable. Any habit you have of wanting and not having is stopping the flow of that manifestation. You can want all day long but all you are producing is more suffering from not obtaining your *wants*.

Lyn: What if I visualize having those desires fulfilled?

God: That works.

Lyn: What if I am grateful for all that I have?

God: That works.

Lyn: What if I plan on receiving my *wants* and make room for it in my life?

God: That works.

Lyn: What if I keep talking about how it will soon be mine, and what fun it is to think about it and enjoy it.

God: That works.

Lyn: I am only supportable if I really do those things.

God: It works when you work it.

Lyn: I work at it part time. You are always what works. And you work full time. I'm going to increase the time I spend with you.

Page 32

Lyn: The more I love and trust you, the more aware I am of your presence. For instance, whenever I see my favorite number, or favorite flower, or favorite color, I know it's your love for me. And double numbers, like 77, or triple numbers like 555 are special greetings.

God: Where else do we connect?

Lyn: I see you in smiling people, in people doing a good job, in people enjoying their day, in kind people talking with me on the phone, in cloud formations and mountains, and in chocolate chip cookies. I don't want to only think of you when I need help, which is out of fear, not love. I'd rather appreciate your generosity and see you as an everyday Santa Claus.

God: I like this conversation. Keep going.

Lyn: I love the times you unexpectedly give me gifts, leaving me nurtured and delighted. And you often interrupt my thinking when it's time to do something, keeping me on time, or in the right direction. You not only give me gifts, but you arrange for me to give gifts, as well. You often send people my way for a simple word, or smile or pat on the shoulder that changes their whole attitude. Mine too.

God: Congratulations on creating a structure that reminds you of love and joy.

Lyn: I want to keep being in contact with you. You're like the sun, always there. Fear and negativity are like clouds, shutting you out, condemning me to gloom and doom. Strange that I spend time with struggle and suffering when you are just a thought away.

God: The more markers and symbols you have for me, the more I show up in your life.

Lyn: Okay. I will continue increasing my love for you.

Page 33

Lyn: I've discovered something very powerful about love. I know that love heals. Love is like forgiveness, letting go of the toxins of hurt and anger, and allows the body to regain its natural ability to function well.

God: Nice.

Lyn: Thanks. I know that love is created *now*, and there is no past to handle and improve. Love is like a delete button. It erases, or rather, there is no memory of anything that bothers me. It's only when I leave the world of love that I become a damaged Lyn, living in an unfair and unkind world.

God: You're doing so well I think I'll take the day off.

Lyn: You're cute. And I got the acknowledgment. Maybe all there is, is love. When I don't feel good I'm disconnected from love, and create a soap opera story in which I star as both the hero and the bad guy.

God: Say more about the bad guy.

Lyn: Oh good, then there's something here to explore. Well, I drag around the times I felt inadequate, or embarrassed or ashamed. Then I think that if people knew how slimy I am inside, they would not like me. And there are times I think that even you might be disappointed in me.

God: Not true. Keep going.

Lyn: If I have no shame when I feel loved or loving there must be two different realities. One is the reality of love. The other is the reality of Lyn—as an identity—separate and distinct from others. When I don't feel good, I'm filled with disgust and loathing about my mistakes and failures. Who I must be in the world of Lyn is living in a graveyard of guilt, shame and blame, trying to look good so I can survive and pass as a good person. It's a good thing you invented forgiveness for we poor sinners.

Page 34

Lyn: Today I am playing *The Perfection Game*. I am declaring I am perfect and live in a perfect world. Rather than improving or complaining, I appreciate my reality.

God: I like this.

Lyn: You taught me to accept and enjoy, and when I do, it's heaven on earth. When my random thoughts and feelings dominate, I'm confronted with problems and upsets.

God: True.

Lyn: Well, since I have only one life to live, and *it is what I say it is,* I say I am perfect and life is perfect. Then I don't have to bother with cleaning up or fixing anything. Why argue with perfection when all is well? I can enjoy each day as a gift.

God: Now you're speaking my language.

Lyn: I thought you'd like this conversation. And thanks for being patient while I work this out. I'm new at the game of perfection and my brain patterns are still filled with the past.

God: How can new brain patterns be created?

Lyn: I can sit quietly and create the vision of my perfect body, perfect health, perfect finances and perfect relationships. I can see the world filled with perfect people, healthy, loving and happy. Happy humans on a happy planet.

God: That's my girl.

Lyn: And you're my boy. Since you're so loving and all-knowing, you would only have created perfection. What if our bodies and lives were designed for ongoing love and freedom, appreciating the good and transforming the bad? On behalf of the billions of people on the planet, thank you for creating us as perfect, living a perfect life.

Page 35

Lyn: It would be good if everyone believed in you like I do. Some people think you are a punishing, judging God.

God: Then they do. Some might believe your faith in me is a misguided fantasy, denying the reality of a hostile world.

Lyn: Uh oh. Yes. I can see their belief is just as true to them as mine is to me. Whatever anyone believes is true for them. But what about when people harm others in your name?

God: They might believe they are defending me, or whatever form of deity or justice they worship. Wars are about people defending what they believe and pushing against those with other beliefs. As are all arguments and disagreements.

Lyn: Wait! I started out by wanting people to know you are loving and now I'm being forced to see that my view of you is just my view, and not necessarily the truth. It's difficult to let others have an opposing experience of you. I love you so much I don't like accepting what I think is a distorted view.

God: Others might think yours is a distorted view.

Lyn: Listen, agree with me that love is the right way to go! Be my partner in letting my beliefs be right for me.

God: Love is the right way to go. Others have their own definition of love. Some believe in harsh love, or a child's view of love, or a more mature view. There is no end to the variety. I love all, whatever they believe, including the non-believers. How could I eliminate anyone when they are all my creations? How could I ask you to love unconditionally if I were to be selective, picking and choosing who to love. I invite you to accept opposing views simply as varieties, like flowers and foods. Differences are good. Making allowances for different views allows you to accept your own thoughts and actions that fail your own standards. The more you love, the sweeter life becomes. See and hear lovingly.

Page 36

Lyn: When Moses asked your name, you said "*I AM THAT I AM.*" I think you were declaring yourself to simply exist. When I say *I am Lyn*, I'm creating an individual. If I say I am that I am, I'm announcing my existence, with no ingredients. Creation can be declaring that *I am*, or *I am* something. I *am* happy, or I *am* sad, is creating it in the world. Saying *I'll try*, or *maybe I will*, or *I'll think about it*, or *later*, is a hit or miss rather than a sure thing. Saying *I am*, gives itself power to reinforce and propel into existence.

God: Give examples.

Lyn: Okay. And thanks for having me work this out. If I think "*I want to be well*," all I'm creating is more wanting. If I declare "*I am well*," I can bring forth the intention and experience of being well now.

God: Say more.

Lyn: Years ago, when I discovered the power of my word, I suffered from an average amount of illnesses and conditions. After creating "*I am always well*," I began to think like a well person. I acted like a well person. The power came from *knowing* wellness was on its way. After a while I became a well person, so I know it works.

God: Does it always work?

Lyn: It only works when I work it. I believe I'm always well, and when my body has symptoms I know my new cells will be perfect, without those symptoms. I don't make a condition or a disease out of it. Occasionally, when I do get sick, I simply believe it's a gift to let go of something that doesn't serve me

God: How's it going?

Lyn: Quite well. I'm an example of being healthy, happy and ageless.

Page 37

Lyn: I've been thinking about age and aging.

God: Say more

Lyn: When young, I judged myself against others, as good enough, or not good enough. I was not good enough.

God: Go on.

Lyn: When I reached middle age, I judged myself against others, to see if I was "making it" or if I was "behind." I was both good enough and not good enough.

God: Keep going.

Lyn: Now that I'm older, I look to see if I'm if I'm surviving or enjoying life. Most of the time I'm good enough.

God: What do you see?

Lyn: Well, I can see the last part of my life seems to be the easiest. The older I get, the less I'm influenced or bothered by others. The measure seems to be health and happiness.

God: What works?

Lyn: *You.* Choosing you as my loving source allowed me to be able to separate sufficiently from the *not-good-enough-identity.* I'm able to create a loving present with less influence from my not-good-enough past.

God: What else works?

Lyn: Love. The loving lady connected to you has a strong enough habit that dims the petty lady in my head that likes to judge and complain. And loving my 37 trillion cells keep me young and healthy. When I have physical symptoms, I look for what negativity or fear I can release. When I have judgements and opinions, I can be uncomfortable enough to recognize the toxic view and take a kinder view. The happier I become, the more I'm unwilling to suffer. The happier I become, the stronger the habit of joy.

Lyn: I heard two bad stories that I have been thinking about for years. Both involve children dying by tragic accidents, and I can't seem to shake them away. I woke up this morning thinking about one of them.

God: What was it about those stories that captured you?

Lyn: They involved children who were adored, whose deaths were accidentally caused by the people who adored them. Those people never lived normal lives again.

God: What keeps those stories alive for you?

Lyn: I can't imagine anything more horrible. An adored child was no more, and the unrelenting guilt and blame was ever present. They were denied that child, and it was their fault. It was the sentencing of suffering that trapped them.

God: How do you think you would have responded if that had happened to you?

Lyn: While I don't think I would ever get over their deaths, or the regret, I don't think I would bury myself with them. Maybe I would form a survivor's group of people with similar stories, to further the healing of all. It's not what happens but our reaction that determines the effect.

God: You would move on in life taking the accident with you as a motivation for love, not for punishment.

Lyn: That's it! The key to why I'm haunted by these two stories is the way those people handled their lives afterward. They saw no way out of their suffering. Since feeling good is my primary intention, I would keep searching for crumbs leading me toward freedom and power. I can now have compassion for their suffering without the agony of feeling trapped with them, and allow release from the upset of those recurring memories.

Page 39

Lyn: Years ago, when I taught fifth grade, I brought two identical plants into the classroom, and labeled one Larry Love and the other Harry Hate. It was an experiment in how emotions affected plants. The class sent loving thoughts to Larry Love and mean thoughts to Harry Hate. By the afternoon, Harry Hate drooped over two inches lower than Larry Love. We were all surprised at how mean thoughts were so powerful. We discussed how making fun of others and teasing can influence them just like the plant.

God: A wonderful demonstration.

Lyn: We talked about how they felt when others made fun of them. We also talked about the times they joined others when they were picking on or bullying another. They said they would not do that again, and many said they would try to stop it.

God: A powerful lesson learned that will serve them in life.

Lyn: The students in that classroom took on individually walking around the schoolyard after they ate lunch being nice to kids who were alone. They shared how much that experience helped them understand people more and how powerful it was to reach out to others, rather than just taking care of themselves.

God: Wonderful.

Lyn: For many years afterwards, when I ran into one of the children from that classroom, they said they remember the love-hate plant demonstration. And talk about it.

God: What did you learn from that experiment?

Lyn: I love my plants, and they are healthy and thriving. I love animals and they often respond to that love. I have even experienced fish in fish tanks responding to my love. I often walk around with a smile and many other people smile back.

Page 40

Lyn: How can I let go of what's bothering me?

God: What makes you hold onto what's bothering you?

Lyn: You're answering a question with a question. Because I'm right, and they or it was wrong.

God: Why else?

Lyn: I hold onto something because I want justice or revenge. I hold onto something because I lost, and I mourn the loss. I hold onto something because it's the principle of the thing. I have a right to remember, to never forget. I hold on to justify myself in some way and blame others.

God: Why else?

Lyn: Aren't those enough? I hold onto something because I think it's the truth and it can become part of me, my identity, my worth. Since it's no longer questioned or evaluated, it belongs to me. Are you going to tell me how to let go of what I hold onto?

God: Why do you want to let go?

Lyn: You should have been a lawyer instead of a deity. I want to let go so it can stop bothering me. I'm tired of being right about what I don't like and blaming those with other views. Instead of being upset about what's bad, I could enjoy and celebrate what's right and what's working. I want freedom and power more than I want to be right.

God: How will you let go of what's bothering you?

Lyn: I let go by forgiving. By reframing. By realizing that that was then and it's over, and I'm the only one affected by maintaining the wound. I can accept that all challenges are a gift from you to discover more ways to experience your love. I can trust that all is well. Okay, I have the power and means to let go. All there is to do is choose to let go. I yield to love and am willing to release what is bothering me.

Page 41

Lyn: It's hard for me to believe you really meant "*Ask and Ye Shall receive.*" No matter how many times you support me, I still wonder and doubt. It shows up as a surprise when the getting is easy. When the getting is hard, I've earned the result without you.

God: We have an interesting partnership.

Lyn: That's just *me of little faith* plugging along, remembering you only when I'm in trouble, or when I stumble into gratitude.

God: We seem to be in a *Lyn is bad* conversation.

Lyn: The things I want are designed to make me happy. Yet getting what I want only makes me happy for the moment. Knowing you love me is my best source of happiness. Maybe I doubt you when I think I'm not worth loving.

God: Most of the time you accept and reciprocate my love.

Lyn: What's interesting about all this is, is I'm a good advertisement for your love. I keep sharing how happy I am, and how great my life is, and credit my relationship with you as a major source. And here I'm complaining about my distrust.

God: Your struggle is just as important as your joy. They each contribute to the whole. You keep increasing your ability to accept loving and being loved.

Lyn: You know, being human is not easy. I wish you had made an easier design for us. It's that free-will thing that's dangerous. I guess it's up to me to figure it out. I ask you to forgive me for the times I doubt myself and transfer it onto you. I thank you for your love and your patience. Mostly, I thank you for loving me when guilt and shame make me feel unlovable. I seem to need love the most when I'm unlovable.

God: Love is always available.

Page 42

Lyn: I think if I visualize what I want I can make it manifest with more power. Is that true?

God: Visualization does have power when you feel good as you visualize.

Lyn: If I'm not feeling good, the negativity compromises my desire. Believing it will happen has the most power. The times in my life when I knew, without a doubt, that I would get what I wanted, I got it.

God: Good. Now think of how you were when the outcome was questionable.

Lyn: Then it was just hit or miss. Not much power or confidence. A lot of hope. And trying.

God: What was the difference in you?

Lyn: When I was determined or intentional, I produced the result. When I was wishy-washy, the result was wishy-washy.

God: Well done. You described *being* you vs. *trying* to be you.

Lyn: Is there a real me and a fake me?

God: There's an authentic you and an inauthentic you.

Lyn: There's a *belonging-to-you* me, and *an-alone-me* struggling to belong to others who also feel they don't belong. I could form Loners Anonymous, except members would no longer be loners. Never mind.

God: Visualize what you want.

Lyn: I see us all living well in a peaceful world filled with happy people. I see myself as a missionary for your love, and as a courier between the worlds of love and fear. I see everyone doing the best they can, leaning toward the light. I see your love inside the sun, sending us all love, satisfaction, fulfillment and joy.

Page 43

Lyn: Does heaven exist?

God: What do you mean by heaven?

Lyn: You know, where everything is filled with love and joy as we visit with all our old buddy dead people.

God: In your world people create their own reality. You see what you expect to see. The same goes for heaven.

Lyn: Go back to we create our own reality.

God: Individuality doesn't exist. It is an illusion. All is one. You declare yourself as separate and make up stories to keep the separation in play. It's fiction writing.

Lyn: I don't exist? I'm not real? I made me up? Then who are you talking to when you talk to me?

God: I'm part of the story that you make up.

Lyn: What would be a good part of the story to make up?

God: You could be an awakening awareness.

Lyn: What would I be aware of? What would I awaken to? Would I discover I'm more powerful than I think I am?

God: You have just asked the perfect question.

Lyn: I think you want me to shake loose from my soap opera of survival. I can think of myself as one of your cells, like one of the cells in my body. Maybe I can see that I'm part of the whole. I suspect I'm rather attached to thinking I'm an individual. But it would be good not to compete or defend.

God: Feeling good is awakening. Smiling is awakening. Loving is awakening. You're on the perfect path.

Lyn: I can ask what God would say and do. I can take on becoming committed, even addicted, to feeling good. I can decide there's nothing more important than being happy. That's a really great idea.

Page 44

Lyn: I want to talk more about how love is always the answer. How can I love when I'm upset? Can I give up my habit of having to be right?

God: You can't love when you're upset. You can only love when you're at peace and feeling good.

Lyn: If creativity occurs from a peaceful space then anything else is correction and improvement of the past. It's only when I'm calm that I can choose my way of being in the present and in the future. Otherwise I'm reacting from past decisions. When calm, I'm an artist with a blank canvas and can create anything. Then I can discover and reinforce until it becomes a habit.

God: Very good. What new habit can you create?

Lyn: The best view is a loving view. If there is something I can do to promote love I am invited to do so. Anything else can be accepted as life's diversity.

God: Keep going.

Lyn: Opinions, beliefs and practices are choices, and it's not my job to use myself as the standard of how others should live. Love accepts we are all your children getting through life to the best of our abilities, however life occurs for us. Coming from love, no one would harm another.

God: What is possible?

Lyn: After an upset, when I calm down, I can know I was just being right, and forgive myself. I can train my brain patterns to think lovingly. Ultimately, that's really what I want. And I know it's what you want for me.

God: You got that right.

Lyn: I got it right when I made you my partner.

God: Love is always available.

Page 45

Lyn: So many changes. So much to talk about. After my husband passed away, I sold the house we lived in for 42 years. I was involved with fixing it up, finding a buyer, and finding a new place to live and moving. I went through phases of fear, sadness, depression and being overwhelmed. Then these wonderful buyers showed up and loved the house. My broker said my energy attracted positive people. After being unable to find another place to live that was satisfying, I sat down and created exactly what I wanted. Within hours I found the perfect place!

God: What are you learning?

Lyn: My past efforts to come from love instead of fear, tend to pay off during times of need and stress. Commitment to feeling good was my best investment with the biggest return. Feeling good is a passive income that keeps producing wonderful rewards.

God: Nice.

Lyn: I remember the moment I decided to sell, feeling unable to go through the storage in closets and garage. A friend came to my house and announced she was going to help me. I said I couldn't do it. She picked up an item and said unless I demanded to keep it, she was going to get rid of anything I didn't love. I joined her in the adventure.

God: Opportunities knock when least expected.

Lyn: Believing in a loving personal God is a brilliant move. I know you're always there, and worth trusting, even when circumstances invite anxiety and concern.

God: Excellent.

Lyn: Since my relationship with you is now a habit I don't stay away for very long, as loving you and being loved by you is too necessary and important. I love you, God.

Page 46

Lyn: I've been thinking about our identities. Our bodies are like machines, designed to sustain life. The body digests and breathes and grows and adapts all the time. It is programmed to survive.

God: Go on.

Lyn: A mouse doesn't wonder why it's a mouse. A giraffe doesn't wonder why it's a giraffe. Humans are the only living creatures that ask questions about itself. Maybe we are higher beings occupying a body.

God: Go on.

Lyn: If the body really is a living machine, it remembers our thoughts and feelings. Happy thoughts are enjoyed and complete. Unhappy thoughts, critical thoughts and fearful thoughts tend to be stored, perhaps for future use. Maybe our machinery repeats the thoughts we most commonly think. I don't think I choose to say to myself, "That was stupid," whenever I don't like what I did or didn't do.

God: Go on.

Lyn: When I'm here, now, authentically present, I create as a discovery. I'm discovering the wonder of life. "Oh, how beautiful, interesting, unusual, etc. When I'm not present, being on autopilot, my body supplies me with my favorite thoughts about what's wrong with me, what's wrong with you, what's wrong with them.

God: Go on.

Lyn: When we accept and appreciate other humans we are peaceful and joyful. When we judge others as different, we separate and defend. The identity might just be a meaning-making machine to run a lazy or resigned mind. I choose to create and reinforce love and wonder, rather than yield to the disempowering thoughts of my frightened child.

Page 47

Lyn: I know I should do a lot of things that are good for me, but I don't. I know I can have it all if I lovingly ask for and expect to get what I want, which is the Law of Attraction. And yet, I spend too much time resenting the lack of what I want, following the Law of Distraction.

God: What else?

Lyn: When I'm happy, I'm being who you created me to be, which is awake and enjoying the moment. When I'm not happy, I am who my identity created me to be, not good enough, wanting what I don't have, and critical of myself and others.

God: You're either experiencing love or experiencing fear.

Lyn: Yes! I'm a little "*Am-I-okay?*" machine, protecting myself like a sardine in shark-infested waters. I'm either Good Girl, or Good Grief. I'm safe connecting with you or feeling good.

God: Is relief in sight?

Lyn: You know, I really am a silly little human. I forget about you and wander into an unsafe world that requires me to be careful. I know the source of freedom and power is connecting with you, especially when I feel vulnerable. Being careful is not present when you're my partner.

God: What else is present when you're with me?

Lyn: Love. Acceptance. Peace. Contentment. Joy. It's the best investment I could make. I'm winning the struggle between my whiny damaged child and my loving capable adult. Connecting with you is a smart move. When I feel good, I'm connected with you. I smile a lot. I smile at the wonder of trees, and appreciate the shape of clouds. I admire the courage of strangers. I smile in the mirror.

Page 48

Lyn: I've been having miracles lately. It feels like you know what I want, and I have been able to receive it.

God: Miracles are allowed in the absence of fear.

Lyn: You wrote, "*Ask and Ye shall receive.*" What stops the receiving after we ask?

God: Reasons. Obstacles. You are either in tune with what you want or in tune with the difficulty of letting it in.

Lyn: How can I be in tune with what I want?

God: Miracles are the result of an open channel, without the cholesterol of fear blocking delivery. You are always in the way when not receiving what you want. You then create reasons to justify why you're not getting what you want, which resists more receiving.

Lyn: When I ask for something it's because it's missing. You can't be saying we should be happy to ask and receive. It takes courage to believe prayers are being answered when gripped by doubt and fear.

God: You have a better chance of receiving when you believe the request is on its way and feel good about it.

Lyn: It's a leap of faith to expect rescue while feeling deprived. It's not easy going from *help me* to *thank you.*

God: A victim needing rescue and feeling deprived is not an invitation for receiving. There's no earning or deserving to have what you want. Be open to ordering and receiving.

Lyn: If I see you as generous and forgiving, receiving would be more natural. Expectation invites receiving.

God: There's no limit to what is available. It makes no difference if you ask for something big or small. Expectation and allowing works. All is well. Ask and Ye Shall Receive.

Page 49

Lyn: We create laws because we're trying to get others to behave in a way that will make us feel better.

God: I'll go along with that.

Lyn: Maybe my judgments and opinions are like laws, made to make me feel better. I say this is good and that is bad. I choose this is right and that is wrong. I vote for this and against that. My life is filled with what works and what doesn't work.

God: I'll go along with that.

Lyn: That's fine except I think about what's wrong or bad and want it stopped. Wouldn't I be better off just to stand for people and things working out rather than trying to fix problems?

God: I'll go along with that.

Lyn: You're doing that annoying repetitive answer thing again. Wait! I just saw something! If I think you're annoying, I drop down the rabbit hole of negative energy in my mind and body. If I see that you're letting me work this out, I feed myself loving energy, and even motivation.

God: I'll go along with that.

Lyn: Now you're testing me. Okay, I know you love me and are guiding me lovingly. It's my job to feel good. And the more I feel good, the more I program my brain patterns to think lovingly rather than critically.

God: I'll go along with that.

Lyn: You go along with anything I do or say. I could use your kind acceptance of me as an example of how I can accept others. I can be a loving observer rather than a judge. Life can be a buffet from which to choose while lovingly leave the rest. Maybe life is perfect exactly as it is.

Page 50

Lyn: I'm angry. Something unfair happened. All I can think of is more reason to be angry, like putting logs on a fire. I think I should put the flame out, but it has a force of its own.

God: You're in your survival mode. You feel vulnerable, defensive, and victimized.

Lyn: You're right. The whole process is full speed ahead like a battleship. I want justice. No, I want revenge. There's no release from this anger that's consuming me. I lost my connection to all that's of value, especially you. I feel unsupported by you, like you don't really care. I'm angry at you for not taking my side.

God: Keep going.

Lyn: There's no light at the end of this tunnel, only helplessness, despair, hurt and isolation. I feel alone in my misery. Misunderstood. Caught in a trap of injustice. Although I want to keep ranting about this, I know I have the power to shift away from this direction, this path, this fire. I'm not ready yet, but I remember that I can choose to let go. I can choose to soften my perspective and restore a gentler view. I know this anger isn't permanent, yet I'm attached.

God: You're at war with yourself, and only you can switch sides. Left alone you will justify your anger, adding more guilt and blame and getting others to agree with you.

Lyn: Anger has power. I'm on a roll. I'm energized. It's hard to jump off the force of anger and think of a softer view. Talking with you helps, even when I'm angry.

God: You can ask me to take away your anger and have you feel loved. You can take a deep breath and feel loved.

Lyn: Thanks for the advice. I'll do that after I've had enough of this tantrum of anger, and remember our relationship. It feels good to choose to be a brat sometimes.

Page 51

Lyn: At times, when I've gotten out of the habit of our electronic talks, I think this book will make no difference so why bother.

God: Thanks for sharing all those thoughts.

Lyn: Thank you for letting me express the ramblings of a confused soul when I'm disconnected from you. I love our conversations, whether in private or for the book and I work stuff out for myself.

God: I enjoy our conversations too.

Lyn: See, now I'm having another series of thoughts about what you just said. Does God enjoy?

God: Say more.

Lyn: If you're giving me your attention during our conversations, don't you have anything better to do? And how can you be available to me 24/7 and still be attending to the business of running earth and heaven? And if I have your sole attention, what about the others? Do they have their own God?

God: Again, let me be a mystery. Faith is knowing without evidence. A belief is just a thought you keep thinking. It's up to you to reinforce what works for you.

Lyn: I feel better when I have the freedom to express fears and doubts about your existence. It's so difficult to keep cynicism, and fear of being conned from interfering with the most powerful and precious resource I have in life. You don't get angry and demand blind obedience. You don't lose patience with me when I fill these pages with how amazingly my life has altered since I embraced our relationship, and then question your existence. Best of all, I don't question your love, a gift that keeps giving. I'll just accept that my mind is doing that thing it does when fearful.

Page 52

Lyn: I have a problem. Most of the time I know problems will somehow be solved, but sometimes I feel overwhelmed and stuck. I don't even think you can help and I feel like a loser asking you for help. I'm afraid you think I have enough. Or I ask too much. Or I remember you only when I want something. Or you think I'm bad and should be punished.

God: I never think those things. I want you to be happy and have what you want. When you feel good you want others to feel good.

Lyn: Sounds like love to me. And useful.

God: It is.

Lyn: Since we're not even talking about the problem, only the resolution, maybe what matters is who the person asking is being. I'm apparently being a miserable victim. I could probably shift from powerless to knowing I can handle this, actively seeking solutions. I could shift into an able-bodied person seeking support. That would be more powerful. And more of an invitation to enlist support.

God: I like how you're thinking.

Lyn: You helped me with my problem, even though the nature of the need was never addressed. This is useful. Anything can be handled. Being stuck and powerless maintains itself. It's a learned disability.

God: You've learned how to fish instead of getting fish.

Lyn: Coming to you for support is a smart move, especially when you don't disappoint or betray my trust. You accept me even though sometimes I complain about your methods. Thank you for your unconditional love.

God: Thank you for sharing your vulnerability.

Lyn: I like that you call it vulnerability instead of shame.

Page 53

Lyn: I want to unclutter. I have lots of stuff from my history that is not useful but has taken up permanent residence. I seem to need to maintain possession.

God: Why?

Lyn: Good question. According to the 80/20 theory we only use 20 percent of what we have. The rest is storage in case we might need or want it someday.

God: What makes you hold onto something?

Lyn: It wasn't so much of holding onto, as unwilling to let it go. It was bookmarked as significant or meaningful in some way. Now that I'm talking about it, I see it was just something I thought was valuable enough to keep. And became clutter.

God: How do you feel about it now?

Lyn: Maybe the value is in letting it go. Holding onto something says that before is seemingly better than today. A keepsake is highlighted with almost sacred importance that makes me the curator or museum guide for the past. Honoring the past is empowering. Missing the past is disempowering. I can be glad it was, not sad that it isn't.

God: What is possible?

Lyn: The more I free myself from the significance of the past the more I can create value from today. And make room for an exciting tomorrow. I can honor the past and value today.

God: What could work?

Lyn: I can set aside time to release yesterday's treasures, making room for today's discoveries. I can pick up a stored item, thank it, and put it into one of three piles: discard, sell or give away. I can make myself comfortable with letting go. It's best to believe the change is already here. I am enjoying my new environment of sweet organization and clear space. Simplicity nurtures my spirit.

Page 54

Lyn: I was angry with someone. I wanted to stop the anger, so I tried liking that person. I couldn't seem to do it. Then I had the thought that the person likes me. I tried it out several times, and it felt good. And the negative thinking shifted.

God: You created a new reality that serves you.

Lyn: Is it possible that I am always connected with love? Sometimes I believe the drama-of-the-moment thoughts and feelings. Life seems to be filled with multiple dramas.

God: Say more.

Lyn: It's not fair. When I'm feeling good I'm free and joyful. Then I sink into a black hole of *poor-me* and *bad-them*. My feelings are hurt, or injustice is done, and I'm in a war zone between good and evil.

God: Good insight.

Lyn: Listen *Oh-Keeper-of-All-That's-Good-and-Holy*, I need a helicopter or a helium balloon to take me away from the gloom and doom. Any suggestions, *Oh-High-and-Mighty?*

God: Listen *Oh-Keeper-of-All-That's Hurtful-and-Unjust*, it takes practice. Notice how much of your time is donated to feeling bad and feeling numb. The more you notice, the more opportunities there are to create loving thoughts. How's that, *Oh-Low-and-Weak?*

Lyn: Ouch. Low and Weak, huh. I'll show you. I'm going to start feeling so good you're going to have to have another category for Feeling Good Stardom. I'm going to start a blog, write a book and make a movie about feeling good.

God: Your star is ready when you are.

Lyn: Until then there's chocolate, or a nice warm bath. I can always visit my neighbor's cat. Or go shopping. Or eat. There's that book, that TV show, that friend to talk to. Or see what's new at the dollar store. If I'm desperate I can read the latest celebrity gossip. Never mind, I don't want the star.

Page 55

Lyn: When I'm feeling good I like what I see, or what I'm doing, or who I am. There's no space between us. Maybe being myself is part of the whole, not a separate piece.

God: When you know who you are, you are awake. When you don't know who you are, you are lost, trying to fit into a survival costume and script.

Lyn: Sometimes I think you expect me to suddenly get enlightened.

God: How about awake?

Lyn: Awake would be nice. When I go away on vacation I wake up and orient myself to what is happening, like a discovery. In familiar places with familiar people I think I already know how they are, and view them as usual, with no interest in discovering who they are today. I'd like to be awake when I speak with others, and even better, with myself.

God: Being awake feels good. It's not a big deal. Sing a happy song, think a sweet thought, smile, laugh, hug. You do feel good much of the time.

Lyn: How come it doesn't seem like I feel good much of the time? Maybe I only notice the down times.

God: Good feelings are natural and often go unnoticed. You measure your struggles and efforts. You notice and collect what you fear.

Lyn: Maybe love is just feeling good, after all. Life seems to be divided into either love or fear. I could pretend I work for a corporation that sells love and my job is to see what's good and what works. When I come from fear I see what's wrong and what's bad and what's unfair. Then I'm working for our competition, fear, who is out to destroy our product, love.

Page 56

Lyn: It upsets me when I've been wrong. I'm invalidated, less than, almost shameful, like a failure. *Love me, love my opinions* is not the way to go. I could use you as my model. You love me just as I am. I'd like to love me just as I am.

God: You're learning.

Lyn: I've been willing to learn. And yet I keep disconnecting, diving into the story of being hurt and misunderstood. What a disempowering habit. That's something I'd like to unlearn.

God: You are discounting the value of suffering. There's a cutoff point when you've had your fill and stop the carnage. You will let it go when it's no longer worth the energy and effort to continue being right about what's wrong.

Lyn: I want to shorten the suffering time and lengthen the feeling-good time. Well, to tell the truth, I am shortening the suffering. I spend more time feeling good than I did in the past. I use powerful techniques, such as forgiving and turning things over to you. When looking through a beginner's mind I discover interest and delight.

God: Enjoying being happy is more useful than feeling bad about feeling bad.

Lyn: I know how to be happy. Life works when I look through your accepting eyes and loving heart. My world is then a gift from a sweet source. Thank you for your love and acceptance, always patient until I join love.

God: You're always loved.

Lyn: I want to do more to feel good. I could see myself as a traffic signal, showing red light for negative views and green light for positive views. I could practice counting my blessings. I could also bless others, couldn't I? Maybe I'll become a blessings counter.

God: Count yourself as a blessing.

Page 57

Lyn: Sometimes truth changes. I used to believe that George Washington was the first President. I later found out someone else was a temporary first President. I believed things were solid until science said that nothing is solid, just packed more tightly. If facts are disputable, then for sure my assumptions and conclusions are probably questionable as well. If my truths can be toppled over, how do I know what to believe? Should I take nothing for granted?

God: To question is to look newly and see with new eyes. The Buddhists call it a beginner's mind.

Lyn: Wait, why are you talking about Buddhism?

God: Take anything from a religion or philosophy or person if it serves you.

Lyn: You know, sometimes our conversations are not easy. You keep pulling the rug out from under me, and then propping me up again. The only constant is that I trust you, and because I trust you and trust your love, I'm willing to let go of much of what I know and consider I don't know much of anything. Perhaps my knowing stops me from discovering and most of what is valuable is yet to emerge. I'm invited to *not know*.

God: An empty vessel and clean slate invite today's eyes and ears to guide today's paths. Become an explorer of new worlds. Innocence and wisdom are powerful lanterns to light your way.

Lyn: I'm going to see if I can be neutral about things rather than taking sides or forming opinions. Maybe that beginner's mind thing is worth exploring. I wonder if I could be neutral about politics. Or about which foods I like and don't like. Or which people I like or don't like. Or which color or season or day of the week or style of clothing, or anything. I could pretend I'm the owner of life and just enjoy it all.

Page 58

Lyn: I'm wondering which is more important, the question or the answer. Questions open investigation and discovery. Answers shut down the inquiry.

God: Not bad for an amateur. What questions interest you?

Lyn: I'm going to ignore that *amateur* label. The questions I like are those that create swiss-cheese-holes in the mystery of life. Who am I? Who are you? Who or what created God? Why are we here? Is there a soul? Is there life after death? Was there something before birth? Is there a heaven? Are we alone in the universe? What is our relationship with other humans, with animals, with other forms of life? Is there destiny? Will life as we know it end? If so, when? Can and should life be extended? As you can see, I'm a question lover.

God: Notice that you don't allow possible answers to stop those questions. For you, those questions are unanswerable. I like how you said mystery.

Lyn: I could do that with everything but you. With you, I require an unbreakable bond and unconditional love. I trust you totally, even though I don't understand you. It's good to trust totally and you never disappoint or betray. I'd rather doubt myself than doubt you.

God: I thank you for your love and trust. You use me for happiness and nurturing, and that seems to be your best answer. You share love with others, using me for refueling. Not a bad arrangement. Thanks for the partnership.

Lyn: Thank you, as well. Our relationship is a great use of the principle of supply and demand. I'm glad you are my unlimited supplier of love. Loving you teaches me how to love others. You really are the best answer to my questions. Okay, I can let all but our love be mysterious. And yet, that might be the biggest mystery of all.

Page 59

Lyn: I'm wondering how was love created? Where is love located before I tap into it? Maybe it's like oxygen, always there. What if love is all there is, and any other emotion is a default response, trying to return to love? Is love a commodity that increases the more it is used, like supply and demand?

God: Keep going.

Lyn: Maybe the purpose of life is to discover love, and we work it out for ourselves. Someone should invent a love mask, like an oxygen mask, and we could breathe in love.

God: Nice.

Lyn: I'm going to keep the love-mask image and breathe in loving thoughts and feelings. Or, maybe it's like a respiratory system, breathing in love and eliminating fear.

God: Say more.

Lyn: Love is not as interesting as drama and fear. Games! We like games. If everyone always won at gambling, most of us would stop playing. Games promise a challenge. We don't know if we're going to win or lose. After winning, we move on. After losing, we stop.

God: Good insight.

Lyn: Good news networks are not nearly as popular as bad news. Stories and action are what sells. The scarier, the better. We are distracted from our own suffering when another is suffering. You should have made love more attractive.

God: Say more.

Lyn: Oh wait! Maybe when we're numb and resigned we need outside stimulation because we don't remember our child-like ability to be interested and delighted with quiet things like nature. I can often use an available tree or bird to release tension.

God: Your natural state is love and joy.

Page 60

Lyn: I was speaking at an event and the leader said I bring light to life. Sometimes, when I'm with another and they experience freedom, I see them surrounded by a light.

God: Say more.

Lyn: Don't know why it's taken me so long to talk about our light. We are all like lighthouses. When our light is on, we can guide the paths of others with love. When I'm worried or complaining, I turn down my light, caring more about enduring and surviving.

God: Say more.

Lyn: I remember a time I was upset when I entered a scheduled event. I took a seat in the rear, not bothering to look for the friend I was supposed to join. At the break the friend came over to me and said she kept looking for me. She saw a woman with my face, but knew it wasn't me, and keep searching for me. Amazingly, my upset shut down the light that was familiar and I was unrecognizable. I decided to be more responsible for the maintenance of my light for the benefit of more than myself.

God: Good idea.

Lyn: I am willing to give up my right to shrink into a resigned, damaged creature living in an unfair, cruel, uncaring world. I'd rather develop the habit of spreading light.

God: Good idea.

Lyn: Thanks. I know what I'll need most is courage. I intend to break the habit of self-survival and to think of myself as a God Junior doing your work here on earth.

God: Good idea.

Lyn: Support me in coming from the power of love, sharing its generosity and joy. Support me in doing my part in keeping my light bright and steady, lighting the way for others to spread their light. Let's let the world glow with love and light for future generations.

Page 61

Lyn: I'm happy. I've been following a food plan my body seems to appreciate. My mirror appreciates it too.

God: You're eating by choice, not habit or defiance.

Lyn: What do you mean by defiance?

God: Sometimes your actions are to prove you can.

Lyn: I sometimes do what I think I shouldn't. Acting defiantly doesn't sound like freedom. It smacks of resistance. Behavior from the past. No freedom. No growth or satisfaction.

God: Yes.

Lyn: Once I'm on track I maintain good habits. For a while.

God: How can you get on track?

Lyn: I can tell you, or someone else, the foods I'm going to eat each day. I did that before and it worked.

God: Creating a support structure is good.

Lyn: Talking to you can be a supporting structure. I know I'll feel good when we're connected. But then again, I can often make plans and not follow through.

God: It's okay when your identity has you suffer and endure. It's just *time out* in life, until you feel good again.

Lyn: Really? I thought I was bad when disconnected. I thought I was bad for being undisciplined in my habits.

God: I never think of you as being bad; you're simply not remembering who you really are.

Lyn: Oh wow! Maybe life can be measured by feeling good or feeling bad. Maybe it's connecting with you versus surrendering to the bratty me, my ego, my identity.

God: You're always loved.

Page 62

Lyn: Can everyone connect with you?

God: Everyone has a connection to a higher level of themselves, whether they believe in God or universal energy or nature or whatever they think exists beyond themselves.

Lyn: Is this a good thing?

God: It is a good thing if you think it is a good thing.

Lyn: I'm glad I learned how to share the burden of living with you. I can turn over the hard stuff and enjoy the sweet stuff. You are my primary love and best relationship.

God: How do you reinforce that?

Lyn: The trick is to remember you. When I connect with you I'm released from the insanity of meanings, guilt, shame, blame, solitude and despair.

God: What else is required?

Lyn: I let go of being right about what's wrong and let go of my arsenal of opinions that protect and defend. It works to believe life is on my side and created for my benefit. I like thinking we're all cells inside you. And that all people are just like me with different stories. histories and views.

God: What do you get in return?

Lyn: I get to know that for this moment all is well. I am well. Life is good and joyful. I get to inspire others with my enthusiasm and excitement about being alive. I get to be a demonstration of happiness bringing good health. By the way, what do you get?

God: I get to enjoy angels at play.

Lyn: I enjoy that you enjoy. Love is a condition and joy is the expression.

God: You're always loved.

Page 63

Lyn: Let's talk about my weight, which at the moment is more important than enlightenment or philosophy. I'm unhappy and I intend to nail this sucker once and for all.

God: Do you want to talk about your weight or your suffering? Suffering is a condition. Weight is your object of suffering.

Lyn: You're not getting it. This issue is a big one for me. I feel if I focus on suffering we're just going to get into some thinking and behavioral conversations that won't make a difference in my weight. I want to be thin more than I want anything else!

God: You're in alignment with *wanting* to be thin, and all you can receive is more *wanting*.

Lyn: Listen, you're still not getting it. When I'm thin I will like myself. I'll feel free and powerful. I'll feel beautiful. Clothes will look good on me. I can wear form-fitting clothes instead of cover-ups. I'll venture out more. I'll show off. I'll enjoy life.

God: Thanks for letting know how it will be when you're thin.

Lyn: I'm mad at you for not helping me lose weight. You probably want me to talk about love and all I want is to be thin. Even though I know it won't keep me happy, I want it. Wow, listen to me! I'm beginning to see that I am at the source of my own suffering and right now I'm not willing to take responsibility for that. It's a relief to tell the truth and not just try to look good. Maybe I'll learn how to love my fat.

God: Talking about it honestly is a good thing. If you could see yourself through my eyes, you would love yourself as is.

Lyn: Okay, that little pep talk was a little calming. It's a relief to be able to have an identity rant from time to time. Thanks.

Page 64

Lyn: A woman asked me what I thought about a friend of hers. I knew it was important to her that I like her friend. I didn't know what to say, since I had a mildly negative opinion. I said I liked the friend.

God: What's the problem?

Lyn: Come on, I lied. Well, I hedged the truth, since there were things I did like about the friend. And, I feel guilty about judging the friend. I want to be like you, accepting others as they are. You're probably not going around with a computer report card giving me bad marks and grades.

God: Right.

Lyn: When I'm not connected with you I become the judge in my reality, usually based on survival. You don't join me unless I come from a loving place so when I'm fearful and judgmental you can't fix it since you don't enter nightmares. Have I got that right?

God: Let's say yes for now.

Lyn: If you can't support me out of my own created *hell*, the surefire way out is to connect lovingly with you and see through your eyes, and feel through your heart. (And no, I won't even mention that you probably don't have a body.)

God: I like the direction you're headed into. Put it all together.

Lyn: Okay. I forgive myself for judging. I now accept my friend's friend, my friend and myself as good enough and worthy of love and appreciation. Okay. Thanks for the trip back home to you and your love. Even though the source of suffering was minor, the subsequent disconnection had the same degree of suffering I experience with something major. The disconnection remains while the reason varies.

Page 65

Lyn: I'm looking at the perspective of "*What's in it for me?*"

God: What is in it for you?

Lyn: As an identity, I feel entitled. I want advantage, accumulation, getting ahead, admiration. My identity lives a life driven by survival and self-promotion. That thinking reflects a less-than person seeking to become a more-than person. I'm not being who I really am and not where I want to be. I suppose I need to know what's available, so I can get ahead to wherever I think it is that will have me make it.

God: What else?

Lyn: Okay, when I'm connected with you and feeling good, I'm fully alive, I don't have guilt or shame or regret. I have freedom and power. Anything is possible. I'm adequate. I'm enough. I've arrived. I'm home. I'm safe.

God: What else?

Lyn: I have a free ticket to freedom and power when I connect with love. Except I call on you only when I remember or if I really need help. Why do I think about "*What's in it for me?*" That's a survival game of being better and special.

God: What *is* in it for you?

Lyn: Okay, I get it. I can stop asking what's in it for me when I start looking at all there already is for me. If I died today and looked over my life, what would I want to see? My identity would probably want me to be rich and famous. As your partner in love, I'd want to make a difference and contribute to others. I'd want all of us to make it, not just me. Each of us can create a stand for all of humanity. I'm taking on "*Everyone lives as a family on a thriving planet?*"

Page 66

Lyn: I want to talk about who I am being when I'm coming from past programming and not being present in the moment.

God: Good topic.

Lyn: There are books written about children having past life memories or memories of being in heaven before they were born. If any of that is true, then when we're very young we're still connected to a higher source.

God: Keep going.

Lyn: Well, we must have lost our *umbilical-cord-like* connection, and discovered we're abandoned, on our own. A lost, confused child would start programming from fear. We would quickly discover we're pathetically unable to take care of ourselves.

God: What are you suggesting?

Lyn: I'm suggesting we created a survival identity to exist, to belong, to be provided for and cared for. We became loud or quiet, admired or obedient, fast or slow, wanting approval or wanting to be invisible.

God: Is that good or bad?

Lyn: It's good for surviving, but bad for allowing for the discovery of who we really are. Let's say we are a little God discovering the power and freedom of creation. An awakening awareness, whose purpose is joy.

God: Anything else?

Lyn: I am going to keep inquiring into how and why we created identity. I want to learn more about what or who is running my show when I'm not creating from choice.

Page 67

Lyn: Each of us has a different view of everything. How can we all get along?

God: You get along when you can accept others as they are.

Lyn: What if they are mistaken? What if they are wrong?

God: You are uniquely you, as is everyone. You don't get along when you don't allow others to be how they are.

Lyn: I want to argue with you and point out there are those that harm, dominate, lie, cheat, steal, and even murder. Yet arguing is being right about an opposite point of view. To dispute is to come up with opinions to support my opinions.

God: Good insight.

Lyn: Thanks. Why is it difficult when another holds a view that is contrary to mine? It's not just another choice, like selecting something different from a menu. When another has different views about life, politics, family, or even food, it feels personal, like I'm being attacked. My sense of self, my worth is being questioned.

God: What would you prefer?

Lyn: I'd prefer to think like you, accepting, loving and patient. I'm going to start asking "*What would God do?*"and "*What would God say?*" and train myself to think lovingly, creating inner peace. You're a good model to imitate.

God: If you were watching animals in nature, you would probably be interested in how they were being. When you observe humans in action, you use *your* standards as a right/wrong scale.

Lyn: Bingo! I'm open minded with nature and judgmental with people. Thanks for the valuable insight. I'm going to see people as interestingly different, like a variety of flowers.

Page 68

Lyn: I don't seem to have enough time to do what I should do and do all the things I want to do.

God: Most of your thoughts and actions are designed to stop you from doing what you *should* be doing. Your biggest distraction is complaining to yourself and others. Being a victim is the greatest distraction from power. Not producing results is your way of defending yourself.

Lyn: I resent that. I work hard. Sometimes. Oh, okay, I do waste a lot of time. I do feel like I'm holding back. I probably don't want to be where I am or what I'm doing. Like a kid being sluggish in avoiding chores. And a lot of what I do is just enough to get by and be good enough.

God: How is it when you're doing what you want to do?

Lyn: Oh well, if it's for me, I can give it my all. Oh, I think I'm starting to get it. I really do enjoy my own little interests. And time flies when I'm having fun.

God: And when you're doing what you don't want to do?

Lyn: I'm sort of a robot with my *should-do's*. No wonder time drags when I am doing something I think I should do.

God: What is possible?

Lyn: It works if I *choose* to do *whatever* I'm doing, and to do it for myself. Do it willingly. Do it because I *said* I would. I might surprise myself by changing *should do's* into *could do's*. I could make it my choice, choosing to do it, transforming a chore into something for my benefit.

God: Your most powerful motivation is choice.

Lyn: The smartest thing I ever do is choose to love you. No, the smartest thing I ever did was to decide you love me. And, to make you my partner.

Page 69

Lyn: Listen, God, I need some serious help. Yesterday my youngest son was diagnosed with a life-threatening disease. I'm reacting all over the place. I keep turning it over to you. Then I get mad at you for letting this happen. Then I become philosophical and put all of life into a manageable perspective. Then I do it again.

God: I'm here for you.

Lyn: Not quite the answer I was looking for. I'm a copy machine that keeps asking *why?* How could it have happened to this wonderful young man? He's loving and kind. Doesn't that count for something in the roll of the dice?

God: I'm here for you.

Lyn: You know, I'm not quite sure what that means right now. How are you here for me? Are you going to cure my son? I think this could be a test. Is my faith in you being challenged? Am I willing to question your existence and powers when something, even something this big, slams me into a wall? Do I just go along for the ride when all is lovey-dovey between us?

God: I'm here for you.

Lyn: I know you are. And I count on it. Thank God for you. Wait, that sounds wrong. Thank you for being here for me. And I believe you are over there with my son as well. I just find it all so difficult to accept. It's bad and wrong and unfair. I have no place to target my upset and fear, so you, the space of peace and joy are somehow at fault. You surely must have the powers to keep one man safe from disease.

God: I'm here for you.

Lyn: Okay, okay, I get it. You're forcing me to rely on who you are for me. No, I'm not going to handle this alone. I am taking you with me all the way, wherever that leads. I love you. I trust you. And I am here for you to be here for me.

Page 70

Lyn: Thank you, God, for curing my son. His recovery was amazing.

God: All things are possible.

Lyn: I was like a tiger protecting her cub. I got on the internet and phone and asked everyone I knew all over the world to pray for him and to ask everyone they knew as well. That tidal wave of prayers made a difference in his healing. Days before his surgery his symptoms eased up. It takes a village.

God: All things are possible.

Lyn: The experience turned out to be a gift, rather than a nightmare. My son became a warrior throughout the ordeal.

God: All things are possible.

Lyn: I also know if the result had been worse, I would have handled that too. I had to accept that my son could die before I was truly powerful in standing for his complete recovery. I even jokingly said, "*God won't let him die or he'll have to deal with me.*" I believe, had that occurred, I would have, eventually, forgiven you.

God: All things are possible.

Lyn: Because I trusted you, I trusted the doctor, the hospital and the whole process. Even though I'm sometimes a controlling lady I felt more in control by trusting you, and therefore believed it was all beneficial. The outpouring of love and support from all directions was a miracle in action.

God: All things are possible.

Lyn: Thank you, God, my friend, my mentor, my love. You are the best investment I ever made. The returns keep coming. Thank you for your unwavering support. His rapid and complete recovery was indeed a miracle. He was not required to do the usual follow-up treatments. He sees his experience as a gift to appreciate life.

Page 71

Lyn: An important decision I made is that the universe is friendly and on my side. It makes a huge difference in having me feel safe and loved.

God: Say more.

Lyn: When I'm challenged in life I can quickly recover, think of an advantage of what happened, and forgive. Not all the time, I admit, but enough of the time to have me feel safe. I reinterpret fearful thoughts into those that make me feel good. I read books or listen to recordings of people with loving views of life.

God: That's supportive.

Lyn: My commitment to feeling good dominates my existence. It's my intention miles above any other temptation or interest. I refuse to suffer for very long.

God: What else?

Lyn: My biggest contribution to others is being happy. Although my accomplishments might be appreciated, none seems to be of more value to others than sharing my goal of being happy. If I can be happy, so can they.

God: I support your quest.

Lyn: You know, having you as my partner is what gives me the confidence to be happy most of the time. When I'm happy I want others to be happy too. Others feel more powerful knowing it's possible to be happy, no matter what is happening.

God: A win for all.

Lyn: We are candles lighting candles. When we're happy, we are your best advertisements demonstrating believing in a loving God is a good investment. When we're vulnerable, others are often available for a hug or helping hand.

Page 72

Lyn: When I don't feel good about myself or life, I want to escape. That's when my addictions come into play. I grab onto patterns of distraction like shopping or eating or computer favorites or wine. I'm getting away with not handling stuff.

God: Keep going.

Lyn: There are people or situations I'm avoiding and what helps me is the seduction of my favorite distractions. They anesthetize the anxiety of procrastination. I don't see them as distractions. They show up as me doing what I want to do rather than what needs to be handled. I'm doing what I want to do rather than being told what to do.

God: You've made my day.

Lyn: I didn't know you had days. Or nights. I thought you just lived on a cloud someplace with an iPad. Or on a hammock. Okay, back to topic. When I take a kind view of what I'm avoiding, I'm free to complete unfinished business.

God: Good.

Lyn: Anything can be handled with you, the path to good health and peaceful sleep. Please give me the awareness and courage to stay in love with you, and stay on task dealing with unfinished business. And I ask you to forgive me.

God: I accept. Ask and it is given. You've asked. Now it is your job to know you're receiving. Envision all is well. Know you're free and powerful, forgiven and forgiving.

Lyn: Maybe you created days to show light and nights for dark. When I come from love, all is light. When I come from fear, all is dark. You are the lighthouse leading me safely home. Home is where the heart is. Or is it the stomach? Maybe it's where the wine is. I think it's time to stop.

Page 73

Lyn: You know I made you up, right?

God: I know how you connected with me.

Lyn: Okay, maybe you do exist, and I just figured out a way to work with you that works for me. Even if I made up that you exist, and now believe that you always existed, I still could be making it all up.

God: Every belief or opinion is made up, whether it seems like you created it on your own, or accepted an outside view as your own. Acceptance is a choice. I am supposed to have created humans in my own image. Maybe humans create me in their image.

Lyn: I see. There's really no way of knowing if you're real or not. And why is this so important, anyway? I'm afraid of being conned. I wonder if I'm conning myself. My relationship with you is so valuable, it's hard to believe your love is unconditional. Believing in you works for me and creating my version of you works for me.

God: For the moment.

Lyn: Maybe. Good thing you're so patient with me. I don't understand how you work. I don't understand how electricity works either, yet I use it to enrich my life.

God: It doesn't matter to me when you question our relationship. Your style is to enjoy inquiring about life.

Lyn: Your love is a lifeline I depend on. Your love and devotion are so strong it makes my dependence on others less important. I forgive myself for questioning you, especially since you don't care when that happens. I wonder if I ponder about you more for the benefit of others who might read this.

God: You'll probably be reading this again yourself.

Page 74

Lyn: Let's talk more about asking. I usually ask when I want you to help me out. Or I'm greedy, and want more.

God: Your frustration of not having what you want clogs receiving. When do you feel generous?

Lyn: When I'm happy I want others to be happy too.

God: What happens when they're needy?

Lyn: That's a tough one. My response is all over the place. It depends on who is needy and how long they have been needy. If it's long term, their need is endless, so band-aiding is probably appropriate. If they are in a short-term crisis, support can be appropriate and rewarding. It also depends on what's going on with me at the time. If I feel needy myself, I'm not generous.

God: When do you ask me for support?

Lyn: Sometimes I'm so caught up in my problem I forget about you. And yet I do often ask for your help when I'm needy. If I have a conflicted response to others when they are needy, do you have a conflicted response to my needs?

God: No, I don't have a conflicted response to your needs. Your asking has a conflicted response to receiving. Your suffering, like being in a traffic jam, stops the receiving.

Lyn: Are you telling me I can't have what I want if I need it?

God: You can't receive what you want when you have reasons for not having.

Lyn: Oh. If I'm ordering from a menu in a restaurant and I have doubts about the food I'm ordering, I could confuse the server into bringing the wrong food. Duh! I'll ask simply and clearly and expect my request to be answered. You keep trying to teach me that.

Page 75

Lyn: I'm excited about what I discovered. Sometimes I bless people. I'm not sure if I'm doing the blessing, or if I'm allowing you to bless them through me.

God: What have you discovered?

Lyn: Silly God. You know everything, so when you ask what have I discovered, you want me to write this down to share with others, so they can know it too.

God: Silly human you're the one writing this. I ask you questions so you can think it through to share with others.

Lyn: Okay. This morning, driving to the market, I started blessing people in other cars and on the streets. I felt a deep connection and love. I continued the blessings as I entered the market. Then I got busy shopping, and didn't notice how different I felt toward others. I was judgmental and annoyed at the long line and forgot an item. I had to go back, and lost my place in line. I needed a blessing myself.

God: Say More.

Lyn: When I'm not connected to you I promote and protect. I'm an independent operator, in business for myself and it's a losing proposition. I'm going to make a bigger effort to connect with you more often during the ordinary moments of the day. Today I discovered the act of blessing is a wonderful way to feel good, spread love and play with you. I know my instant connection is when I feel gratitude or appreciation. I then become my higher self, more in your higher rent district. I'm moving my address closer to heaven.

God: Bless you.

Lyn: And bless you! Whatever that means.

God: It means we're both blessed.

Okay God, Let's Talk

Page 76

Lyn: I don't want to. You can't make me. No, I won't. I'm not supportable. Locked in. Locked down. Locked out.

God: Well now, Miss Resistance. What seems to be the problem?

Lyn: You. You're the problem. And so is everyone else. I don't want to do what I need to do, what I'm supposed to do, what I should do, and what I'm not going to do.

God: Okay, don't.

Lyn: No, no! You should tell me to do it. Don't you get it? It needs to be done! Time is running out! Fast!

God: You think you're in trouble. You're stuck and think your world is falling apart if you don't start doing it.

Lyn: Yes, yes. That's it. Thanks, at least, for understanding. And can you understand that I'm a victim of my own *"Nobody's going to tell me what to do"* Especially me. So, *oh wise and wonderful one,* can you help me out here?

God: I don't think so. You're a lion at your own gate. Want sympathy?

Lyn: No! You don't believe in sympathy. Compassion is more your style. And you have no sympathy for a pathetic, stubborn lady behaving like a child yelling "NO" to everything.

God: I give you permission to rant and rave, feel guilty and be stubborn and scared. Come back to me when ready.

Lyn: You're sneaky. You know that's annoying and irritating. If I were available, that might have some power.

God: Take a deep breath and let love in.

Lyn: I'm still resisting but it was fun ranting.

Page 77

Lyn: I seem to be a robot acting out orders from before. My thoughts are like a kaleidoscope shifting through my history with worrisome fears taking over my viewing screen.

God: Nice observation.

Lyn: Listen, oh wise one, are you going to help me out here? You're my last resort. Oh wait! Why are you my last resort? Shouldn't you be my first resort? How is it I only come crawling back to you when I have no willpower and am drowning in guilt and shame?

God: Nice observation.

Lyn: Okay, let's see. I am run by past habits. I don't want to be run by past habits. What are my choices? I can notice what I'm doing. Noticing is a beginning point of power.

God: Nice observation.

Lyn: I see you're doing that repetitive response thing you do sometimes. Maybe that's a bad habit you could try to overcome. Are there therapists in heaven?

God: Observation not so nice.

Lyn: Okay. I notice what's wrong. Now I'm at choice. Do I continue in that bad direction or handle what I'm resisting? My tendency will be to continue in the bad behavior, and yet it is possible to change my mind and do the right thing.

God: Nice observation.

Lyn: The right way is the one that comes from love, not covering up fear. I can do this. I can create brain pattern habits that come from love. It would make me feel good, and produce the results I want. It's a no-brainer. And I could turn it over to you when I'm tempted by the bad thing. Yes, I will create good thoughts today that will become the pattern for tomorrow.

Page 78

Lyn: I like helping people solve problems. Now I'm a little uncomfortable for having given advice when I wasn't asked.

God: Were you telling them what to do or sharing a good idea?

Lyn: Oh, I see what you mean. I think it was a little of both. I shared what I liked and then said they should do it too.

God: Then your generosity was mingled with domination.

Lyn: Too bad. That's not my intention. I guess my enthusiasm felt like pressure. Should I apologize for telling them what to do? Does apology always work?

God: Often but it depends on your purpose. If you apologize to save yourself, it could seem superficial. If it's to have a loving relationship, it could melt the differences.

Lyn: Are purposes or intentions known to others?

God: Good question. What do you think?

Lyn: I think in some ways we know where someone is coming from. We can sometimes feel when they're for real, or trying to sell us something. Not always, though.

God: What is possible?

Lyn: I could say everything that comes my way is beneficial.

God: That could work.

Lyn: I thought you'd say that everything *is* for my benefit.

God: Everything that comes to you really is in some way for your highest good. Life is on your side.

Lyn: That feels good. Maybe everything that comes to anyone is meant for their highest good. Then our most difficult lessons are our greatest gifts. Maybe being peaceful allows us to accept challenges. I know that partnering with you is a certain path to peace.

Page 79

Lyn: When I have petty, even cruel judgments about others, it leaves me unsafe, living in an unsafe world.

God: How is your view when you're not judgmental?

Lyn: I see what's good, kind, generous, beautiful and loving. I see a world that's an invitation, not a threat.

God: Will this conversation make any difference in the future?

Lyn: Isn't this insight sufficient for growth?

God: Only if you take action. Insights can be fleeting.

Lyn: It's not easy to notice when I form a judgment, since I think it's an informed opinion. More like the truth.

God: Do you feel the same when you appreciate and when you notice problems and flaws?

Lyn: No. One makes me feel good. The other makes me a bit unsafe. I do feel uneasy when I gossip or judge.

God: Good observation.

Lyn: Maybe the person to feel good about is myself. When happy, people don't need to reduce others to feel better about themselves. Happy people see the good in others.

God: Remember that *"Do onto others"* thing.

Lyn: Thanks for the reminder. When I see others as the same as I am, neither better nor worse, I can treat them the way I want to be treated. That's a game worth playing, I'm also going to play the appreciation game. It has the benefit of making me feel good and others feel good. We're all looking for love and appreciation anyway. It's a win-win for all.

God: Nicely done.

Lyn: I have a good teacher. And a great model.

Page 80

Lyn: I discovered a new game, and I'm excited about it. You'll like it.

God: Tell me about it.

Lyn: Gratitude is a favorite or yours. Research says gratitude reduces stress, increases health, and improves relationships. Happiness is appreciation for the ordinary.

God: I like this.

Lyn: Although I know gratitude works, I keep forgetting to be grateful. I've been looking for ways to remember. And then I figured out a way to trigger gratefulness.

God: You have my interest.

Lyn: It's called the *Thank You* game. I've started saying *"thank you"* to myself, for no reason. Since thank you is a response, I then automatically look for what I'm being thankful for.

God: How's the game going?

Lyn: Amazingly well. I love it. When I go to sleep at night I say, *"thank you"* and I appreciate the gifts of the day.

God: What else?

Lyn: When I eat, I say *"thank you"* and it awakens me to the gratefulness for food, how it tastes, and how it was prepared.

God: What else?

Lyn: Before an activity, I say *"thank you"* and appreciate the opportunity, rather than have it be automatic. I have a new appreciation for my car, my clothes, my family, my country. I so appreciate my *"thank you"* bringing me more aware of the courage of people and the beauty of nature.

God: I like the *"thank you"* game.

Lyn: Thank you.

Page 81

Lyn: I arrived! I arrived! Hallelujah, I arrived!!

God: Say more.

Lyn: I've spent my life hoping to *make it*. When I've made it, I will have arrived, instead of trying to get there. I thought when I had enough love, I would have arrived. I wanted enough health, enough wealth, enough respect, enough success to have arrived. The goal was to be happy enough to have arrived.

God: What happened?

Lyn: Well, this morning, I woke up joyful. I was filled with the joy of being alive and the privilege of having a body. I was hugging myself, and smiling. Fulfilled and satisfied, I had the thought, "*I have arrived!*"

God: Congratulations.

Lyn: Thank you. It wasn't an accident, you know. I don't want to take all the credit—and of course I do—but it was my determination to experience heaven on earth. I wanted to know it was possible. *Arrival* is not something fixed or stationary, but a home base for visits and retreats.

God: Well done, my child. Well done.

Lyn: Thank you. I don't want to give you all the credit—and of course I do—but it was our partnership that made it possible. Could my long search be over? I have arrived. Not like I died, or stopped. I have the experience of making it, getting there, winning the Oscar and Emmy and Olympic medal. My life will continue, with the difference being I've already won the game of life. I can enjoy the rest of the ride without having to prove myself. There's nobody I need to please, or anything I need to accomplish. My love tank is full and my award table is crowded. My life is complete.

Page 82

God: Wake up. Accept that you are God.

Lyn: Not yet. I don't want the game to be over. I like being separate, trying so hard and through drama, effort and suffering to return to you.

God: You are me.

Lyn: Not yet. Not if I continue to believe there is a difficult journey to get to you. A long, arduous journey, filled with stories and agonies of biblical proportions. I'm not ready for the game to end.

God: Why?

Lyn: Good question. Why *am* I avoiding being God? Is it more fun to have the game be discovering I'm God? I'm attached to the identity I developed to survive being separate from you.

God: Love is magnificent.

Lyn: I know. Maybe I'm setting up the delight of discovering I'm God, like anticipating the wonder of dessert at the end of a meal. Or being addicted to the game of finding happiness, finding love, finding a purpose in life. Searching for love and happiness is a game I like to play.

God: Home awaits you.

Lyn: Not yet. I'm a rebellious child who escaped to the candy store and doesn't want to leave, even though the candy store is hell, suffering, survival and loneliness.

God: You are me. I am you. All is well. All there is, is love. And loving like God loves is a great game to play.

Lyn: I'm like the child that rewraps a gift so she can unwrap it again. Maybe the purpose of life is to love, not to be loved.

Page 83

Lyn: I'm giving notice to my identity. Enough is enough! I'm unwilling to spend the rest of my life traveling between the realities of my identity and who I really am.

God: Interesting.

Lyn: Listen, I say I want to be your partner, and yet I keep falling into the sinkhole of my past programming which is based on guilt and shame. It's as if I have two different sets of clothing. One is elegant and simple while the other is flashy, to get attention, or different, to rebel or get sympathy.

God: Say more.

Lyn: I'm looking at how to support my ability to stay present to our connection and be of use to others rather than be dominated by my own survival. I came up with a plan.

God: Do tell.

Lyn: I'm cleaning up my environment, getting rid of extras that I store. I'm only keeping clothes I like and use, and anything from the past that nurtures me today. I'm unwilling to be a storage facility for used-up yesterday.

God: You can also create space in your mind to allow love and appreciation more visiting opportunities.

Lyn: When I tune into your radio station, I align with your loving view and joyful appreciation.

God: How can I support you?

Lyn: Help me let go of the past to be here now, present, feeling good. Please send reminders that leash-jerk me back to innocence and wisdom when my past hijacks my mind into thinking I'm a not-good-enough Lyn.

God: Done. A clear space and a clear mind allows us to connect and you can be home for longer and longer visits.

Page 84

Lyn: Got any tips for being happy?

God: The Ten Commandments.

Lyn: I know about those. Any others?

God: Lyn, we've been talking for a long time. If you were to make your own list, what would that say?

Lyn: Okay, here goes:

1. Know that you're loved.
2. Trust that life is on your side.
3. Be grateful and appreciative.
4. Give your word freely, and keep your word.
5. Forgive.
6. Be of service.

God: Nice.

Lyn: I really believe those are worthwhile. And, it's a good idea to remind myself of my own values, from time to time. I'm just not making enough effort to reinforce their message. Or worse—like the Ten Commandments—those rules are for saints not folks like me.

God: Any other tips for being happy?

Lyn: The irony of this conversation is that I'm a loving and decent person when I feel good. My word and actions are coming from a satisfied person rather than one trying to get somewhere. When I'm happy I make a difference. I don't need rules then because who I am being is a contribution. When I'm not happy I'm not-enough and life is not fair.

God: What tips for being happy are available now?

Lyn: Feel good. Do whatever it takes. Create another view, forgive, appreciate. I can ask your support in being happy. I can take your loving view with me.

Page 85

Lyn: I want to work something out with you about *now* and *time*. If there is only now, everything else is a moving story. We created an identity to survive being human. My identity is called Lyn, a sometimes-whiny-brat filled with fear, judging everyone and everything. She made up a story of her history.

God: Go on.

Lyn: When I exist *now,* I'm awake in heaven on earth. All is well. When I think there's a past, I'm in hell, suffering from a graveyard of past hurts, regrets and disappointments.

God: Go on.

Lyn: This feels big and important but my brain patterns dealing with my past keeps taking over my awareness.

God: Keep coming from love. Enjoy the trip.

Lyn: Yes, I've thought of that. The spirit is willing but the flesh is weak. NO! The spirit is willing and that's all I need. I'm willing to live in the *now* more of the time.

God: Where's the catch in your last sentence?

Lyn: Time. If *now* is all there is, is there time? Although in this accepted reality, time exists. When I feel good I'm powerful and all is well. When I don't feel good I'm not in *now,* but in the past, or rather programmed by the past. Uh oh, I'm getting lost trying to stay focused here and now. It's like trying to hold onto sand. I'm either awake or trying to be awake.

God: Theories and explorations are useful. Experience is what counts. Enjoy the wonder of who you are and what is possible. Interest and curiosity about who you are is what makes you human. No other creatures question themselves. All that matters is the view from love.

Page 86

Lyn: Life is unequal and unfair. You really shouldn't have given us free will.

God: I created you in my image. When you are being the person I created you to be you are loving and accepting.

Lyn: I think I disobeyed you like Adam and Eve. Out of shame I created a not-good-enough, different, special me.

God: Say more.

Lyn: As a survivor my thoughts are about me. I'll be generous after I've made it. But of course, my identity never makes it. I can never be good enough, smart enough, rich enough or secure enough to have arrived. When I see through the eyes of a survivor life is competitive and unfair.

God: Keep going.

Lyn: Dominated by past judgments I live a default life, waiting for the world to motivate my interest and passion. When condemned by my past I'm just enduring my existence, needing drug-like habits to occupy my life. I distract myself from guilt and shame. It's not easy thinking I'm bad, a loser and a failure.

God: What is possible?

Lyn: I have choices. I can bring myself to this moment. I can choose this time, this place, this person. I can be here, tasting food, appreciating the wonder of having a body, the wonder of nature, the wonder of the diversity of people. When life is seen through eyes of love, I'm loved and safe. When free, I'm delighted. Love is simply enjoying anyone and anything. I'm either loving you or trying to get your love, somehow. I'm looking for something that's not missing. I can allow your love to comfort me.

Page 87

Lyn: You're mean. If you loved me, you'd give me what I want.

God: You are mean to yourself. I love unconditionally, and yet you won't let my example of love be the model for you. You use fear to expect the worst and complain about not receiving the best. You become hurt and angry with others, wondering why you're sad and lonely.

Lyn: Oops. I apologize for saying you're mean. I know it's me. I judge others and hold grudges. I compare and compete. I want more for me than I want for others.

God: You play the blame game.

Lyn: Oh. I think you're right. I blame politicians and restrictive countries and global warming. I blame injustice and unfairness and thoughtlessness. I fill my thoughts with ongoing information about what's wrong with them, with life, with me. But shouldn't I care? Isn't that loving?

God: Fear is never caring and loving. Fear separates and defends. Fear creates more to fear.

Lyn: Okay, I see the problem is me and the solution is me. I now forgive myself for thinking of what's wrong, rather than what's right. I forgive myself for being interested in problems, rather than appreciating the perfection of it all. I forgive myself for taking a limited, petty, microscopic view of life, rather than the telescopic view of *all is well*.

God: Good work.

Lyn: I promise to be a better messenger of your love by being grateful for your love, your generosity and your guidance. I can teach by example. When I love you, and others see I'm healthy and happy, they might be interested in knowing my secret. I love you, God. A lot. I can share with others that you are the source of my happiness.

Page 88

Lyn: While I certainly feel connected to you when I write, there's an automatic editing going on as well. Where is the line drawn between being appropriate and being inauthentic? Am I being myself or trying to impress or influence?

God: Say more.

Lyn: Oh, I just saw what bothers me. I write in sentences, but I think in snatches. Maybe that's why I was concerned I was being insincere or disingenuous.

God: Everyone is insincere when not coming from love.

Lyn: Oh well now, that cuts it down to size. Maybe I can use feeling good or not feeling good as a measure. Although there are times when I don't know if I'm feeling good or bad.

God: Feeling good has joy and belonging. Feeling bad has defending and protecting.

Lyn: The truth is, I love our talks, and they make a difference in my life. My wish is that those who come across our talks feel themselves included and loved.

God: Sharing what you love is a gift to those on that path.

Lyn: When I think of what there is in my life that has the most value and gives the greatest return, it's you.

God: Thank you for sharing our relationship.

Lyn: I want to give others an example of a loving personal relationship with you, and, if interested, they can design their own fit. If they're not interested, they probably won't be reading this anyway. With you I'm never alone or bored or doomed. Since our relationship offers me so much, you're too big a gift to keep to myself. Loving you is the biggest jackpot of all time.

Page 89

Lyn: I need your help. There is something I need to handle, and, although time is running out, I'm not handling it. I'm distracting myself and resisting.

God: Do what you need to do.

Lyn: Can't. Won't. Not going to. Sorry.

God: No problem. Anything else I can help you with?

Lyn: I guess not. I suppose what I really wanted was for you to do it for me. Could you help me if you wanted to?

God: Could you if you wanted to?

Lyn: Hmm. That's a good one, big fella. Yeah. I guess I could, even would, do it if I really wanted to. What I really want instead is not do it. Want to talk about anything else?

God: Nope. There are better things to do than listen to you whine and complain.

Lyn: Ouch! That hurt. That's not like you at all. Are you messing with me to shake me out of my cynicism and despair?

God: Is it working?

Lyn: Maybe. I am sort of considering just starting the stupid thing and getting it over with. This is the closest I've come to being able to do it. I know that once I get started, it's not so bad. Thanks for your help, I think.

God: Is there a lesson here that's useful?

Lyn: Yes. All it takes to go from a no to a yes is to take another view. Defending and standing firm is just me acting like a two-year-old thinking nobody's going to tell me what to do. Even me. I can shift my rebellious child into a useful person by taking your hand and enjoying love's abundance.

Page 90

Lyn: I want to thank you for taking over a burden I've been worried about. I turned it over to you, and kept turning it over whenever I started suffering. My burden lightened. I have no idea why I ever worry when it's so easy to turn it over.

God: The problem you turn over never really existed. Suffering is an illusion created by a lost frightened child.

Lyn: If I turn all my worries over to you, would I be happy?

God: Yes, if you release the worry and feel good. No, if you harbor doubt and fear.

Lyn: I think it's natural to be concerned about myself.

God: You disconnect from your source, thinking you're special. Only those not good enough need to be special.

Lyn: Wait a minute. If I thought I were good enough, wouldn't I still want to be special?

God: Why?

Lyn: For attention, I guess. To stand out from the crowd.

God: When you're happy, you enjoy life, and there's no need to demonstrate your worth.

Lyn: It all boils down to just plain being happy. That seems to be the cure for everything.

God: That's about right.

Lyn: I'm creating that I am happy. I know that works. I am happy. I am a happy person. I know how to return to happiness when I leave. My experience of happiness increases with each day. I am so happy I teach happiness.

God: I am happy to know it.

Page 91

Lyn: After the initial honeymoon period of a new love, intensity, and even interest often diminishes. Maybe everything diminishes unless reinforced.

God: Say more.

Lyn: When love stops being created we're disappointed, Love promised happiness, and didn't deliver. It couldn't. Love had the couple see the perfection in each other, and all was well. The couple then stopped seeing perfection and started seeing their own hurtful past played out in the other. The other is blamed for changing or for having fooled them.

God: Say more.

Lyn: When you experience loving another, you're safe and able to be happy. When you need another to *prove* they love you, you keep proving they *don't*.

God: Say more.

Lyn: It's all too complicated. I just want to be adored and cherished forever without having to earn it. Or compete for it. Or lose it. Am I asking too much?

God: No, not from me. But yes, from others.

Lyn: I'll settle for you adoring and cherishing me for now. Maybe if my love tank is filled with your love, I can come into life fully loved and won't market for more love and approval. I can probably be satisfied with you as my love.

God: Know you're loved. Allow it. Trust it. Enjoy it. Appreciate it. Be responsible for *knowing* you're adored and cherished. Life is a gift meant to be enjoyed.

Lyn: The joke of life is looking for love outside, when it's inside. I lose when I expect others to love me more than I love myself. When I look at others through your loving eyes, I enjoy and appreciate how unique and amazing we are.

Page 92

Lyn: When world events invite fear, how do I create peace?

God: Notice where peace exists, as in kindness. You get what you measure for. Look for peace and you'll find it. It's like ordering an item from the menu.

Lyn: The problem is drama and sensationalism catch our attention.

God: Say more.

Lyn: People in the Western world think people in the Eastern world are restricted. People in the East think people in the West are driven crazy by activities.

God: What world view would you like?

Lyn: Most people are kind to each other. They do the best they can with how their culture and families are structured

God: What else?

Lyn: We all want to love and be loved and be known and accepted. We want to make a difference. We want to live in a world where differences are allowed and variety is appreciated.

God: What else?

Lyn: It's not what happens, but our reaction to what happens. When focused on good things, we change our patterns of thought to those of appreciation. Good happens when good is expected. Good invites more good.

God: What else?

Lyn: The world is at peace.

God: Good job. For more happiness love the unlovable.

Lyn: That would make it easier to love myself.

God: You are always loved.

Page 93

Lyn: I've been looking at the distinctions of giving and receiving - two types of giving and two types of receiving.

God: Say More.

Lyn: Giving from identity has a survival purpose. I *should* give is not your choice, and is then experienced as *being taken from*. When we're present generosity of things or service brings joy to the giver as well as the receiver.

God: Say More.

Lyn: Receiving from identity can satisfy momentarily, before yearning for more, better or different brings dissatisfaction. Receiving when we're present in the here-and-now is a gift. When I'm feeling good the getting is a sweet hug.

God: Say More.

Lyn: People who give all the time, can experience burnout. When tired and unfulfilled, it doesn't feel like there's anything left to give or care about. Then the giving has stopped, and it becomes a burden. Living with or working for people dominated by survival can be unsatisfying unless we create satisfaction, choosing to do what we are doing, with joy.

God: Say More.

Lyn: When actions or thoughts are mechanical, we are left depleted rather than nurtured. To-do lists, homework, work, or care-giving require refilling, like gas to a car and food to a body. We are responsible for filling our love tank. If not, our not-good-enough or not-worth-loving takes over.

God: Well done.

Lyn: I guess we can say feeling good is loving, and not feeling good is just living. Being present in the now has us be real, like a diamond, while just being mechanical in getting things done is just bling, like a rhinestone.

Page 94

Lyn: Sometimes, when I think about some terrible injustice I feel bad and helpless. It shows up in my memory and I relive the injustice and am uncomfortable.

God: The experience is incomplete.

Lyn: Well, today I was speaking with someone who was upset by another's behavior, and it stays with them. I asked how it made them feel about themselves. They said not good enough and helpless. I then asked what it reminded them of in their history and they came up with a youthful upsetting incident.

God: I like this.

Lyn: I asked them to forgive the perpetrator, taking a kinder view. I suggested they see that misbehaving person as a plant, leaning toward the light, but probably bending from shame and fear. They lash out, expressing their own lack of power by dominating others. Happy people don't need to inflict pain.

God: Nice.

Lyn: If we can have compassion for the unlovable we live in a safe world. If we see everyone as simply on their own path we have more compassion for ourselves when we violate our own standards of behavior. We can forgive us all.

God: Amen.

Lyn: That's the first time you said that. Amen is really a closing statement. I guess you really meant for us to follow "The Golden Rule" of doing onto others as we would have them doing onto us. You know, that sounds fair.

God: Amen.

Lyn: Okay, you made your point. I will love others more. When I love anyone, maybe the world benefits.

Page 95

Lyn: Do you ever get angry?

God: Anger is an emotional reaction *against*. I'm not against anything. Love generates more love.

Lyn: You should be concerned about human suffering. You really should. There are injustices, you know.

God: Suffering is not accepting. If you choose to resist, that's your business, not mine. If you let life be the way that it is, suffering would stop. Injustice is when you disapprove.

Lyn: Shouldn't we help others?

God: If that's what you want to do, go right ahead.

Lyn: Shouldn't we fix things if life isn't fair?

God: Fair is relative. Accept that life isn't fair and be happy.

Lyn: I can't believe there isn't something I'm supposed to do. There must be some purpose in life, like making a difference.

God: Love, kindness, and acceptance make a difference. When something is bad and wrong we want to fix and improve. That's just bringing the past into today to make better. What if you come from accepting life as it is and creating that which enhances and empowers life?

Lyn: See, in one way, you had it easy. Since you were the first, you didn't have to compete for the God job.

God: You have the fearful Lyn compete with the loving Lyn. It could be easy if you knew you were godlike, and you could enjoy and create anything. You are the first to be you. Be a trailblazer in being the unique you as a gift.

Lyn: The loving Lyn thanks you for what I see, feel and think. The fearful Lyn asks for your support in handling uncomfortable sights, feelings and thoughts.

Page 96

Lyn: I was talking with a friend and she said something I didn't agree with. I started arguing with her. I stopped in mid-sentence realizing I was getting upset that she disagreed.

God: Good observation. Saved a lot of arguing time.

Lyn: Now I ask myself why I need to be right.

God: I ask you the same thing.

Lyn: Objectively, I can accept that people have different opinions, different lifestyles, and different viewpoints so why can't I calmly accept when someone disagrees with me?

God: Excellent question.

Lyn: Okay, generous creator of it all, you're going to make me work this one out with no help from you. I think my opinion takes on a personal investment. It's not just an opinion. It's the truth. I know it's the truth and if you question my truth, you are attacking me. You are suggesting I'm wrong and stupid. I can't let you win. I'm at war. My life is at stake...over a silly opinion that I could change if I didn't feel attacked.

God: You're getting to a vital element in humanity.

Lyn: I think so too. But what's the answer? Better yet, what's the question? I think one question is, "*Why do I have to be right?*" Another question is, "*Should I give up being right?*" "*How can I give up having to be right?*"

God: Excellent questions.

Lyn: See, right about now I'd like you to jump in and take over. I feel like I'm in over my head. If having to be right is a humanity issue, surely you must know the antidote. Oh wait, it comes down to LOVE. Love is the answer.

Page 97

Lyn: I have been suffering over an upset. I keep forgiving. Then I remember the upset and I'm off into suffering.

God: To forgive is willing to let go of suffering.

Lyn: I thought forgiving means to let go of what happened. Maybe letting go releases the hold of suffering. I wonder what keeps pulling me back into the rehashing of words and events.

God: You are unwilling to accept what happened.

Lyn: Why is it always me who needs to change? How about making them change? How about helping me out for a change?

God: I am helping you out. You refuse the workable solution. You want to be hurt and angry and still want peace.

Lyn: I just realized that I want you to inject peace into me, like a drug, taking away unpleasant feelings. I think I have a fantasy view of your powers.

God: You have a fantasy view of your lack of powers. You feel helpless in altering circumstances. Taking a kinder view softens limiting judgments, allowing the drama to disappear.

Lyn: I often visit the playground of past wounds. I seem to be more attracted to drama than peace and tranquility. Just when I feel like an unenlightened dummy, you treat me like a developing child, who is loved no matter what.

God: You're always able to discover the path home to love and peace. Dealing with conflicts is an invitation to use your higher self as a resource.

Lyn: Thank you for your constant patience. Suffering certainly is a waste of time when you are just a prayer away.

Page 98

Lyn: I want to talk about focus. When I concentrate on something I'm present in life and discover more. When I'm not focused, my mind wanders like a moving kaleidoscope.

God: True.

Lyn: I see why people meditate. A clear mind has more ability to concentrate. I don't meditate, even though it's a good idea.

God: True.

Lyn: Stop agreeing with me, and help me out.

God: What is your request?

Lyn: Help me focus more.

God: How do you propose I do that?

Lyn: Okay, you don't insert yourself. What is it you do again?

God: You want my job description?

Lyn: No, that's ridiculous. You created us so we must be useful for something. Maybe we're little God Jr.'s discovering love. Maybe we're training to be big Gods.

God: Maybe.

Lyn: Love, or just feeling good, creates an experience of being here and now and stops the clutter of the past. Being present in life gives us the innocence of a child and the wisdom of the ages. When my mind rehashes the past I lose concentration, awareness, and yes, focus.

God: You asked me to help you focus. Trust that I am helping you. If you think your prayers are being answered, you're available for more support. Have love exist like a layer of ground under whatever you're looking for.

Page 99

Lyn: When I decide there's something or someone that will make me happy, I do what I can to make it happen knowing I will be happy once it arrives. All is well until I get what I want.

God: Then what happens?

Lyn: The satisfaction with the accomplishment is short-lived. I'll either start taking it for granted, or count the ways I'm disappointed. I start to feel more stuck than satisfied.

God: What's the problem?

Lyn: The problem is thinking something outside of myself, like achieving or accomplishing will bring satisfaction and fulfillment. And will last. I think it will make me happy.

God: Say more.

Lyn: I keep forgetting I am solely responsible for being happy. I think it's luck or earned or deserved. The world as I know it, is misinformed. Happiness belongs to those who see happily, think happily and feel happily. Some people think a lack of suffering means happiness and satisfaction.

God: Go on.

Lyn: Real happiness is joy. Feeling good for no reason. The happiest among us enjoy the moment, the beauty, the wonder, the sweetness of who we are and the world we live in. It's a partnership with life, knowing we belong, we count, are accepted, and known and enjoyed. Life is on our side.

God: And then?

Lyn: Then whatever happens can be an opportunity to feel good. Instead of being a challenge life can be a gift. We can live life being happy. Sharing with others how they can be happy enhances our capacity for happiness. Love lights the way to happiness. We are candles lighting candles.

Page 100

Lyn: With you, I'm being with a powerful loving friend. I become larger, more available and fulfilled. You're always there, on call. I'm active, like a co-creator, instead of passive like a victim. Believing in you is a good idea.

God: You treasure what you think is valuable.

Lyn: I love my decision to make my relationship with you a primary value in my life.

God: You also think our relationship is of value to me.

Lyn: Yes, I sure do. It works to think you love our relationship. Since I want to be happy, thinking I make you happy makes me happy. Without you, I keep looking for love on the outside rather than on the inside. With you, my happiness supply is full.

God: What else?

Lyn: With you, I live in the world of love and abundance, rather than the world of scarcity and limitation. Without you I would spend my life marketing for love and approval. I would always lose, since looking for love means I'm not loved enough, and probably not worth loving.

God: What else?

Lyn: I think you love me, no matter what. Before, when I thought you judged me, I thought you had a report card filled with bad marks. Now I know nothing would have you stop loving me.

God: If you knew how loved you are, it would all sound silly.

Lyn: Sometimes I know that. Sometimes I feel like your partner on earth. Maybe humans are missionaries for love. And the payment would be to keep sharing joy.

Open a Page.
Choose the possibility of
and easier or kinder view.
Allow your inside love to
warm your heart and
sweeten your days.
Welcome love.
It works.

For more, visit
http://www.lynlevine.com

Made in the USA
San Bernardino, CA
22 March 2018